NON-FICTION

NON-FICTION

UEA MA
Creative Writing Anthologies
2022

CONTENTS

ANDREW KENRICK & FREYA DEAN Foreword	VII
IAN THOMSON Introduction	IX
KARINA CHEAH dénouement...	2
CATHRYN FARR Of Farrm and Family	8
ERIKA FIORE Looking For Water	16
CHARLIE GARDNER I'd Rather be at Work	22
EDWARD GRIERSON Crocodiles	28
SARA KATSCHKA They're Coming	34
JENNIFER KNIGHTS An Interview	40
HANNAH MURGATROYD Disabled Dread	46
CANDACE PIETTE Manaus	52
DAFYDD POWELL HALLS Clippings	58
JUDY REITH Gone	64
TINA ROCCHIO Prolonging Loss	70
EZRA JOHN WOODGER INT. LIFE – DAY	76
Acknowledgements	91

ANDREW KENRICK & FREYA DEAN
Foreword

It doesn't seem so very long ago (six years, in fact) that we were in the same position as the authors featured in this anthology, coming to the end of an intense year of reading and writing, saturated with words and stories. So much so that, at the end of it all, many of us felt reluctant to return to the 'real' world, we wanted to remain immersed in all these wonderful stories – but how?

One of the things students often struggle with as they arrive at the end of a course is 'what to do next?' As writer-students this question of what next features heavily, but takes a slightly different form: the pressing concern is what next for the work you have just completed. The manuscript that you have spent 12 months or more honing and shaping and re-working until it really says something in exactly the way you want to say it and, as such, deserves a life of its own out in the world.

With fiction, it always seemed to us, this route to publication was clear: there were ample (paid) opportunities for the submission of short stories, allowing writers to build a reputation (and perhaps a career) before aspiring to publish their first novel. However in the UK there were far fewer opportunities of this kind for writers of non-fiction, and certainly no dedicated venue for short, creative non-fiction pieces.

And that's how our magazine, Hinterland, was born; first conceived in emails sent between essay deadlines and hurried conversations in the Enterprise Centre between seminars, given a life of its own as funders, bookshops and – most importantly – writers started to take us seriously. Our intent: to provide a platform for new and upcoming writers of non-fiction to submit and see their stories published – and get paid for it too. When we started the magazine we looked ahead to the first four issues, hoping we'd make it to the end of a year. Thousands of submissions, a nationwide reach of stockists as well as our own webstore, an ever-growing community of subscribers and upwards of one hundred published pieces later – many by first-time authors – we have just released Hinterland's eleventh issue. And it's this latter group – the writers, both published and unpublished

– who really fill us with encouragement, whose trust that Hinterland might be the right home for their story makes it all worthwhile.

We are, of course, biased in saying so, but for us no other genre possesses creative non-fiction's potential for storytelling and experimentation. Whether memoir, essay, psychoscape, food or travel writing, or work that straddles genres and can prove deliciously impossible to define, there are stories within non-fiction more compelling than even the most outlandish works of fiction. There is no creative material more wonderful, more powerful than the truth.

And just as truth is the animating force behind many of the stories featured in a typical issue of Hinterland, so it is with the stories presented in this anthology. Between them they showcase the range and power of creative non-fiction to translate the raw material of the everyday into something that sings on the page.

So how will these authors answer the question of 'what next?' Well, we don't think they will have to wrestle with that question for long – we look forward to reading more stories from them over the years to come: whether as full-length books, online articles and essays, or perhaps even as features within the pages of a non-fiction magazine.

Andrew Kenrick & Freya Dean
Founding editors, *Hinterland*

IAN THOMSON
Introduction

Creative non-fiction can accommodate any number of disciplines – the personal essay, travel reportage, memoir, confession, anecdote, wiki page entry, aphorism, poetry and – why not? – film script. It does have to show literary potential, though. Otherwise it would be *non-creative* non-fiction (which is not what we want.) If I had to define the genre, I would say: 'true stories well told'. Creative non-fiction is, really, the literature of *fact*. That said, many of the authors in this anthology consciously borrow from the devices of fiction. They create action-heavy scenes, or scenes that include dialogue, or scenes with vivid description, or a combination of all three.

Any piece of writing necessarily involves a fashioning and re-shaping of events. (The etymology of the word *fiction* is from the Latin *fingere,* to 'mould', 'shape' or 'contrive'.) We do not expect non-fiction to distort in the way that fiction does, but of course it *does* distort. Most good non-fiction writers make life more interesting than it is, as they blur the distinction between fiction and truth-telling. In his celebrated Edwardian memoir *Father and Son,* published in 1907, Edmund Gosse recounted conversations that purportedly took place when he was a prepubescent child. Had the conversations been made up? Certainly they had.

The shape-shifting, ambiguous nature of truth is a theme explored by some of the non-fiction writers here. Ezra Woodger, in his absorbing film script 'Int. Life-Day', considers his troubled teenage self and asks if he really was like that, or was that how others *perceived* him? There is always a special risk when putting a family member (let alone oneself) into 'self-biography', as Samuel Taylor Coleridge called memoir. Tina Rocchio's 'Prolonging Loss', a sour-sweet meditation on the Alzheimer's that has transformed her father utterly, nevertheless moves the reader.

When is a life worth telling? In her starkly moving 'Gone', Judy Reith considers the last four days of her husband's life, as he lies dying in a hospice. The piece is a marvel of unsparing lucidity. Death – the final insensibility – runs like the black line in a lobster through Erika Fiore's 'Water', a celebration of her adored older brother, who died some years ago by his own hand. (Fiore is not afraid to address weighty religious themes.) Cathryn Farr, in 'Of Farrm and Family', vividly reconstructs the events leading up to a shooting on her land in Western Washington. (Fortunately no one was killed.)

A flavour of the essay (from the Middle French *essai,* 'to try', 'attempt' or 'experiment') runs through the anthology. Edward Grierson, in his charming 'Crocodiles', brings to life the reptile houses he visited and came to love during his childhood. In 'They're Coming', Sara Katschka looks at her abiding interest in zombie movies and the fear they generate in her. (The piece frightens like an unlucky number.) Elements of travel writing distinguish 'Manaus' by Candace Piette, about the Amazon rainforest's enduring 'mystery' and the European gold-diggers who descended on that part of Brazil in the Victorian heyday. The world is of course a much smaller place today.

Karina Cheah's semi-experimental 'dénouement...' asks (among other things) where home is for her in the digital age: Penang? Bangkok? Or Maryland, USA? Closer to home, in 'Trimmings' Dafydd Powell Halls describes a visit he made to a Turkish barber shop in Norwich. (The polyglot hair-cutter Yusuf, we learn, comes from a long line of barbers back home on the Anatolian peninsula.) A different part of East Anglia is the setting for Jennifer Knights' spirited meditation on the life and times of a 'semi-retired' clown who lived in a caravan beside the River Bure in the 1970s. The piece is lit up by a fetching wry humour. More grave, in 'I'd Rather be at Work' the environmentalist Charlie Gardner contemplates the inaction and empty words of governments in the face of the climate crisis. Resistance holds the key to saving ourselves, he maintains.

All the pieces derive from conscious craft, and I mean that as a compliment. Often, the easier and more effortless a piece of writing looks, the more difficult it has been to write and the more thoroughly it is underpinned by technique. Of course all good creative non-fiction contains an element of ineluctable mystery – it is 'great' in ways that are not always easy for us to fathom – but still hard graft counts for much. Hannah Murgatroyd's powerful 'Disabled Dread', an amalgam of personal anecdote and memoir, radiates a documentary authenticity and emotional rawness in the telling. The anthology is a book to treasure.

Ian Thomson

This diverse anthology comprises the latest work from the 2022 cohort of non-fiction writers studying UEA's renowned Creative Writing MA.

KARINA CHEAH

Karina Cheah grew up in Bethesda, Maryland (USA) in a multicultural Southeast Asian household. In her writing, she explores intersections – between people and place, between culture and identity, and within the self – and is especially interested in how we learn to exist in the spaces these intersections create.

karina.cheah.1@gmail.com

dénouement...

> 1. *An excess of chai lattes, biscuits, and cakes. The gentle hiss of steaming milk and soft clink of china in cafés. Exchanging ideas and pages with friends, commenting on a sentence here, a word there. Wading through the fog of nothing to write about or, in other cases, having too much to say. Late nights at my desk, on my bed, on my floor in the company of the clicking laptop keys beneath my fingers. Words turn to sentences that turn into paragraphs, appearing on a blank page.*

In my writing, I turn inward, trying to make sense of strange events and past traumas. It brings a perverse sort of joy – not only in the drive to untangle tension, but in the act of writing itself. There's a curious excitement that comes with leaning into internal conflict, of watching words describing feelings I've always had appear on the page for the first time.

Rarely do I settle in to write something without tension. Something happy. In my first-ever creative nonfiction workshop, my professor said: "It's hard to write about happiness and make it compelling."

I wish I remembered that scene more clearly. Perhaps, since I still remember the sentence from four years ago, it does not really matter. I enjoy tackling puzzles with words – like why I still ride horses after my friend died in a riding accident. Why I struggle with piano performance anxiety even though I love to play.

Happiness on the page doesn't come easily. I cannot tell if it's because it's truly difficult, or because I haven't dedicated myself to trying.

> 2. *Words on pages – stories read and reread, with new things learned from each visit. Words between people discussing the passages we read and what we learned from them. Reading spots: tucked under a blanket on the couch, outside on the grass. The soft rustle of pages turning. Character arcs encompassing love and loss, mystery and discovery, conflict and resolution. Interior Chinatown, The Lord of the Rings trilogy, Black is the Body, The Faraday Girls.*

"Happiness threatens the things that every writing workshop demands: suspense, conflict, desire," writes Leslie Jamison. "It's not crying out for expression because it's not looking for anything, whether resolution or sympathy."[1] She adds that this "asymmetry" is true in reading as well – it's more interesting to read about something being wrong than everything being right.

Yet too many wrongs can overload the reading experience. *A Rumor of War,* on veteran Philip Caputo's experience in Vietnam, exposes some of humanity's ugliest moments in brilliantly crafted prose. In every chapter, the writing was so vividly horrific, so relentless, that I could only read a few at a time.

My favorite books strike a balance, doing what I like literature to do – reflect elements of the real world. *The Faraday Girls:* Love alone does not make a happy family. *Interior Chinatown* was the first book to tell me that the Asian-American experience – valid, messy, and complicated – exists outside America's binary of "Black and White."[2] From *Black is the Body:* I will always carry the burden of representation. My favorite real-world element from *The Lord of the Rings* is that the hero does not succeed alone.

David Ebenbach points out that there is nothing wrong with writing about darkness, just as there is also nothing wrong with writing about light. To ignore the world's richness and complexity – to decide that only one makes for interesting writing and reading – would be a lie.[3]

> 3. Bangkok: humidity like cling film on my skin. The high glint of the sun over the pearly pagodas of วัดอรุณ. Overhead: the rattling of the SkyTrain. Looking for my uncle, ลุงโม, in the crowded 'Arrival' hall at Suvarnabhumi Airport. The smoky taste of noodles and rice in ก๋วยเตี๋ยวคั่วไก่ and ข้าวผัดปู; the blend of glass noodles and vegetables and the crunch of เปาะเปี๊ยะผัก. Fruit and dessert: มังคุด and ข้าวเหนียวมะม่วง. "Do not squish" signs in mango crates at Gourmet Market. Snatches of Thai in the air, swift and musical – words I do and don't know.

---

1 Leslie Jamison and Adam Kirsch, "Is It Harder to Write About Happiness Than Its Opposite?" The New York Times, March 11, 2014, www.nytimes.com/2014/03/16/books/review/is-it-harder-to-write-about-happiness-than-its-opposite.html.
2 Borrowing a play on words from the novel. The protagonist, Willis Wu, has a role in a crime TV show called 'Black and White' with a Black actor and white actress as the leads.
3 David Ebenbach, "Why Write a Happy Story?" Gotham Writers, n.d., www.writingclasses.com/toolbox/articles/why-write-a-happy-story.

In writing on being half-Thai, I tend naturally toward the "sense of wrongness."[4] Being allergic to peanuts, a staple ingredient in many Thai recipes. Struggling to learn the language because the tangibility of my connection to Thailand is scrambled without it. Here lie paradoxes to pick apart and tensions to untangle, the things that every writing workshop demands: suspense, conflict, and desire.

Yet for every difficult moment in Bangkok is an uncomplicated one, the kind that "collapses characters into people who look just like everyone else."[5] I hear unfamiliar Thai words and ask my mother for their meanings to grow my vocabulary. I've had far more well-cooked Thai meals – where you can just taste the smokiness of the wok on rice or noodles like grill lines on a burger – than close calls with peanuts.

At my aunt and uncle's house, they spar jokingly over their outdoor cat, my aunt wanting to keep her well-fed and my uncle saying he's sure she can provide for herself. They join my parents, my sister Kanitta, and me for our usual conversations – school and work, family affairs and international politics. It's for these ordinary moments that the four of us will make the annual twenty-hour journey from DC to Bangkok, even though flying is the opposite of our idea of fun.

> 4. Penang: the light brush of the coastal breeze lifting water droplets from my skin. High-rises on the island's northeast corner and the mainland's bumpy coastline across the Malacca Strait, as seen from Gurney Drive through hazy air. Searching for murals in the streets of George Town with Auntie Beng Choo. Red envelopes on a kitchen table – delayed Chinese New Year gifts. A pandan dessert, eaten roadside at a rickety table. Snatches of Cantonese, Hokkien, and other languages I don't recognize; Malaysian English on all sides. The collective protest when Granny orders what seems like far too much food for the table, before we vindicate her by eating it all.

We haven't made this twenty-hour journey in four years. Pandemic and all that. I am anxious to return, because Bangkok and Penang and the family I haven't seen are sinking in my memory, sensations growing fuzzy, images blurring around the edges. Surprising, then, how many quiet, joyful moments I can unearth when I put my mind to what remains. Perhaps, when there are so many, it is hard to single one out.

4 Jamison and Kirsch, "Is It Harder to Write About Happiness Than Its Opposite?"
5 Ibid.

Maybe that's what always made it more difficult to write about Penang. No sense of wrongness, no suspense, no conflict. We move from moment to moment as a family, lacing each one together with an excess of dim sum and the stories we still have to tell.

Would these pockets of happiness be compelling? In workshops, I've both asked and been asked to linger in the detectable moments of narrative tension. Something has to drive the piece forward. Does that preclude a moment of joy from simply existing on a page, the way it does in my memory?

> 5. *Conversations over dinner trying to explain a 'Karen,' discussing the dog's diet, uncovering bits of family lore.* The Economist *magazines spilling from the kitchen table to the side tables. The red pot of Dada's mac and cheese waiting on the stove. Mama's crab cakes. On the wall above the blue couch: Kanitta's four-panel painting of the sun over the sea. Moose curled up on the couch, his tail thumping on the cushions when he sees me. Framed photos, two dried corsages, and the model horses from my childhood on the shelves facing my bed.*

Home is the house where I grew up in America – in Bethesda, Maryland, perched on a hill at a street corner. It's the ten-minute walk from the Friendship Heights Metro stop and the increasingly gentrified shops on Bethesda Row, where the ghost of the Barnes and Noble haunts the Anthropologie that took its place. It's the narrow wooden bridge over Little Falls Stream and the evolution of the playground at Westbrook Elementary School.

Home is arguments about ordinary things, like who should be eliminated from this episode of *The Masked Singer* or whether my dad should be giving Moose this many treats between meals. It's inside jokes, like Kanitta and me alternately saying "egg" several times in a row when someone is making eggs. Late-night conversations in any given room, the lights low. We are a happy family.

There is no such thing as a *perfect* happy family. I learned that from *The Faraday Girls*. Kanitta and I have explained how it can be difficult to be at home, how we sometimes struggle to break free of the roles we grew up in – the kind of tension that writers love to interrogate. Where did these roles begin? Why do we, now adults, still fall into them?

These questions would build narrative conflict, but to place conflict at the center of my family life would be a lie. The beauty of home is that we are always in *dénouement*. For only a short time each year, every bedroom is occupied, and the dim warmth of fairy lights seeps from the cracks under our doors. Moose barks softly from someone's bed, paws twitching in his sleep.

> 6. *An excess of inside jokes. Quotes out of context on Post-Its and in phone notes. Group texts sharing news when we're apart. Animated conversations in cafés, in living rooms, in kitchens about books and writing and general happenings. Reminders of people: the rings I wear, strange photos of cats, diagrams of molecular structures. Memes exchanged on social media platforms. Photos on walls in every place I've lived.*

My friends and I meet up to be in each other's company. We exchange gossip, stress about work and finances, complain about politicians, and decry the state of humanity. That's tension, of course, but not between ourselves. In the same conversation, we take a misspoken word or unexpected turn of phrase and run it into the ground, feeding off each other as we descend into our bubble of hilarity. Does it create narrative tension if no one else thinks we're funny?

In the same outing, we quiet down with our laptops, books, and headphones. We tap our fingers on the table and stare into different points in space as we individually untangle our own little tensions – the emails that have piled up, the solution to a chemistry problem, the meaning of an unfamiliar word. Companiable silence hangs in the air between us, tethered by the comfort that we are all at work, together.

It is hard to write about happiness and make it compelling. So difficult, in fact, that in trying to write on things that make me happy, I have also written on writing about them. Used this to create tension, conflict, a narrative arc – something to drive the piece forward. Could these moments of joy have simply existed on the page, the way they do in my memory?

Ebenbach, David. "Why Write a Happy Story?" Gotham Writers, n.d. www.writingclasses.com/toolbox/articles/why-write-a-happy-story.

Jamison, Leslie, and Adam Kirsch. "Is It Harder to Write About Happiness Than Its Opposite?" The New York Times, March 11, 2014. www.nytimes.com/2014/03/16/books/review/is-it-harder-to-write-about-happiness-than-its-opposite.html.

Yu, Charles. *Interior Chinatown*. New York: Pantheon Books, 2020.

CATHRYN FARR

Cathryn Farr is an adventurer, wife, mother, grandmother, memoirist. Her writing bridges understanding, sharing what readers may never experience, but which will broaden perspectives. Cathryn writes simple joys and complex turmoil found in families and communities and believes our stories, shared while sitting knee-to-knee, have power to unify the world.

CathrynMFarr@gmail.com

Of Farrm and Family

I married Ross Farr in 1991. By 2004, our family included six children and we had bought a lovely 5-hectare farm in Western Washington where we raised chickens, milked cows and tended organic gardens. We called it The Farrm. This excerpt is from a working manuscript that traces my decision, as a mum and grandmum, to arm myself with a gun.

—

We moved to Gig Harbor back when there was one stoplight and one bridge to the peninsula. Its narrow, winding streets are densely lined with fir and cedar, hemlock and spruce, with seasonal displays of colour from apple, maple and dogwood. A drive skirting along the many water inlets reveals keyhole views of rocky beaches and green pastures. You may hear the shrill piping of a bald eagle soaring above the water or the honking of Canadian geese as they travel in V-formation. Mists rise over the bays and evening settles into night and before you know it, you are lost in the dark, since there are no streetlamps.

A visit to The Farrm takes a full 20-minutes of S-curves and back-tracks once you cross the Narrows bridge. Turn off the main road at the grange. The hilly golf course will be on your right. Wind past several side streets that nestle neighbourhoods you'd never know lie behind timber-wooded walls. Enjoy yourself; float your arm out the window and let it ride the waves of the wind. Smell the salt water alternating with evergreen. When you've just about given up getting there, that's when you meet the 'T' in the road. If you turn to the right, you'll find Island View Market, a waterside boat landing, country store and pub. Our youngest daughters, Tsia and Cathryne, love to walk down to buy candy with their best friends, our nearest neighbours. They'll sit on the bench by the dock, watch the gulls, talk about boys, and build the courage to swim to Dead Man's Island at low tide.

Turn left instead; drive a couple miles through trees that form a canopy above your head. The road follows a saltwater inlet that a hundred years ago ran and spawned Chinook salmon. Reverentially, the trees bow away on the right to reveal a small valley. The inlet has narrowed to a stream that runs through the middle of waving green pastures. Eight farmhouses are spaced along the west; a tall forested ridge behind them rises like crenelations on a castle wall. Ours was the first homestead here.

The cement footings in the giant red barn are dated 1925. Save for the new roof and cement slab floor, the barn remains as it was built nearly a century ago. Logs were harvested from surrounding forests and crafted to create the beams that span the length and breadth of this huge structure. It has stabled steaming work horses after a day of hauling and stanchioned hundreds of heifers as they were milked. Each fall, tonnes of hay were stacked in the hayloft and it kept secret the best hiding places of the children who played there. It remembers the boys climbing amongst the rafters, the girls swinging in the doorway. The barn welcomed the swallows, owls and bats who made their homes here and was friendly with so many barn cats, so many mice and rats, so many dogs. And now us.

The original two-storey farmhouse was razed and rebuilt in 1991. Now its high ceilings and tall windows with north, east and south exposure invite the pastoral world inside with us. There are no curtains; we don't need them. We see only one house when we look across the front pasture, half-a-kilometre away.

Every room of the house has its own prospect of the farm. The side door faces the driveway, garden, and the barn, but we always call it the front door; two metres tall and all glass, held in a wood-frame I painted ironstone blue. This is the entrance we use most often. The one I open and yell for the kids, but only the dog comes running. The one that if you weren't careful would slam so hard it seemed the glass would break, until Dad tightened it. The one the dog stands at with his nose pressed against, begging for someone to come out and play. The same one the grandkids use half a bottle of glass cleaner washing. It measures all our comings and goings. It sees us off for morning milking, greets our friends, and checks teens arriving after curfew. It is in the background of family pictures.

It is witness to our most terrifying moment.

24 OCTOBER 2013, 4:15 PM
ROSS (HUSBAND AND DAD)

The family is waiting for me in the house to begin Tsia's birthday party, but there's a truck coming up the drive, so I step out of the barn and wait. The driver is a stranger. He is bald, sports a gang-styled neck tattoo and is wearing an over-sized jacket. Through his passenger window, I ask how I can help as I command our dog to stop barking. He tells me he's looking for a family member and needs directions. I warn him to stay in his truck – the dog bites – as I duck into the barn to grab a map. When I return, he has left his truck and is walking around, peering into the cars in my driveway.

A wave of wariness hits me as I hand him the map and he turns from me without looking at it. With no compunction that I am observing his movements, he walks toward my house and stands, scanning the windows. A sickening premonition continues to build in my gut.

What is this guy thinking?

He's not in his right mind, possibly on something; he has avoided eye contact and is oblivious to respecting private property. I am aware he outweighs me by two stone, and his bulky coat potentially hides weapons. I remember his decorated neck.

Sensitive not to provoke him; I wait and watch.

I feel some relief when he finally gets in his truck – but then he asks,

'Is that your house?'

'Yes, that's my house.'

'Is that your family inside?'

I scowl. My patience with this intruder has lapsed.

'I gave you the map you need, now it's time for you to leave.'

He sits in his truck.

I stand by the barn door, watching him.

A full minute passes.

I again urge his departure.

He's alternately looking at the map, then at the house and ultimately tosses the map onto the passenger's seat, exits his truck and heads straight for my front door.

My family is behind that door – my wife, my children and my mother. I realise, too late, that I should have positioned myself more defensively. This man, erratic and with unknown capability and even more opaque intentions, has decided to enter my home. I manoeuvre through the parked cars between us and shout as I try to catch up:

'Stay away from my house – don't you go in my house – Do NOT go into MY house!'

He takes the front porch stairs two-at-a-time.

I unholster my sidearm and rack a round into the chamber as I run. I have him in my front sights; my mind agonises in slow motion:

Are you really going to shoot this guy?

I really want time to think this through. Is there no other way?

There is no time – he's opening the door and going in – my wife – my children!

He opens the door, and steps inside.

I pull the trigger.

NOELLE (DAUGHTER, AGE 16)

My younger sister Tsia was showing us what Grandma had bought for her birthday when I heard the shot and a tremendous thud and my dad yell, 'I told you don't go in my house!' I thought someone must've been playing with my dad's gun and accidentally fired it. But that absolutely wouldn't have happened because my dad is super responsible with his gun. My dad even cussed at the guy – and he never cusses – so I knew something was seriously bad.

Dad yelled, 'Call 911' and I was closest to the phone so thought, 'I get to do this!' but then suddenly realised I had no idea what to say so I handed the ringing phone to Mom.

CATHRYN (WIFE AND MUM)

Who dared to pop the birthday balloons?! I hate being startled!

I turn to yell at my son, Seth, for bursting the balloons thinking,

Wait – I didn't buy balloons!

Instead, I see blood pooling behind a man writhing and groaning in my hallway.

My previous trajectory to kneel beside the man flows into flight for the phone.

Noelle has already dialled and hands it to me. I turn and face the scene once again as I hear,

'911, what is your emergency?'

'My husband just shot a man. In our home.'

25 OCTOBER 2013, 4:15 PM

Twenty-four hours ago, my husband shot Brandon Bird just inside our front door. My ears are ringing and my arms are heavy. I can't string my thoughts together; nothing seems to makes sense. But I have been up since 5:30 a.m., have resumed my regular routine, and now I am sitting in my kitchen, trying to conjure up dinner for our family; my elbows on the table, and my hands cradling my head, just feet away from where Mr. Bird had fallen and bled.

My husband joins me in the kitchen. I stand and we embrace.

He holds me a long time.

'I'm hungry, I'm just going to grab something.'

'I'm not sure what there is, I haven't made anything. I can't really think.'

'That's okay, Love, I'll grab something.'

He opens the fridge, and outside the dog begins to bark. We freeze. My body is flooded with adrenaline, a sensation I will experience randomly for most of the next year; our eyes meet and reveal my new relationship with PTSD. The dog-alarm sounds because a vehicle enters our driveway. My husband peers out of the window as I cling to his side. Suddenly, we live in a fish bowl. I am frozen as my husband moves to intercept what my nerves have decided is another threat.

Ollie's booming laughter enters our home before he does. He is a retired Seattle police commander and has been our friend for close to ten years; my shoulders release their tension and gratefully receive his big bear hug. His wife, Renee, wears a serious smile; her eyes full of concern, her arms bearing dinner.

IF DOORS COULD TALK

During the next month, sensational yet scanty reports were aired. Before the detectives had even left our home that night, reporters were calling for interviews. I was desperate to guard what little of our privacy I could, so with anxiety mounting to unbearable, I unplugged the phone.

We discuss buying curtains or blinds – of moving. The memories of life on our Farrm will go with us, but the front door I painted ironstone blue, will stay.

Like the barn, the door has stories to tell. Stories of love, of laughter, of resolution, and like the barn, of reaping and sowing. It has welcomed friends and family after a day of work and play, and has protected our family of eight as we slept. This fall, chaotic commands echoed through its doorway and it keeps transparent the effects of the percussion that pierced flesh and home. It remembers Dad's decisive actions; his children gaping and sobbing in the hallway. The door opened to medics and detectives who made their case here and was privy to so many choices, so many questions and voices, so many fears.

The door now finds itself, for the first time, locked, day and night. The children no longer run in and out without checking in and out. The dog's nose smudges the window from the inside.

The barn holds its own secrets in the loft, but the door remains open and transparent.

ERIKA FIORE

Erika Fiore grew up in Southern California where she became a teacher and then worked with Holocaust survivors in Los Angeles. During her MA at UEA, her writing explores the idea of wrestling with God in a memoir about losing her older brother to suicide while they were both undergrads.

erika.shayne17@gmail.com

Looking For Water
An extract from a memoir

I had what felt to me a prophetic dream three days before my older brother, Salvie, died. It was 2009, and we were both living in San Diego, California as university students. We had moved into a two-bedroom apartment in a sunny, outdoor complex called, *Trieste*, named after a port city in Northern Italy. The name of our building sounded close to the word *triste*, which means "sad" or "mournful" in both Italian and Spanish. Being half-Italian and half-Mexican, coincidences such as these and dreams collided into an unwanted fate. I sometimes had dreams where the spiritual and the material blurred more clearly.

I was walking alone through our apartment complex. It looked like it had been abandoned for years and was overgrown in post-apocalyptic vegetation. I stepped over dark dusty leaves, green moss, and vines that crawled along the outdoor hallways, clung onto the building walls, and draped thickly over ledges. The outdoor walkways that connected each apartment floor to its corresponding parking structure level sprawled like human catwalks. Salvie was on one of them. He was wandering through the complex as well, but in a less aimless kind of way. I looked to him.

"What do we do next?" I said. "What has become of this place?"

"It's not safe here," he said, looking at me, "We need to leave."

Salvie moved towards a thick, metal pole. It went up from the concrete walkway into the sky above us like a giant beanstalk. I looked up to where it disappeared into the shifting gray clouds. I felt thirsty.

"Salvie, I need to get some water first," I said and looked around to see where I might find some.

When I turned back, Salvie was already climbing up the pole about 20 feet above me. He couldn't wait for me. And I couldn't follow him. He soon disappeared into the overcast sky.

TWO YEARS EARLIER, 2007

Salvie was an aerospace engineering student at the University of California, San Diego (UCSD). For a while, he shared an apartment with one of his best friends in the university town of La Jolla. Since my school was only 20 minutes away, I often drove to visit Salvie and relax in their apartment. We loved to have movie nights on the weekends. Salvie drove me to the La Jolla Blockbuster, which doesn't exist anymore. It was blue and gold inside, lined with white shelves covering the walls and short aisles with DVDs. There was a tempting section of candy bins by the registers, but the prices were usually higher than those at the supermarket.

The Blockbuster was bustling on Friday and Saturday nights. Salvie and I split up to collect our movie candidates. Then we showed each other and decided which one to pick – sometimes we rented two. Occasionally we chose a new movie, but we often gravitated to classics from the 80's or 90's like *The Patriot* or something funny like *The Goonies*.

After checking out, we drove into the shopping complex across the street for treats. The Ralphs in La Jolla had an aisle lined with clear plastic dispensers filled with every kind of candy: chocolate covered fruit, chocolate covered nuts, caramels, and gummies. Even when Salvie and I went to Ralphs for actual groceries, we found ourselves in the candy aisle every time as if by magnetized instinct. Once we realized where we were, Salvie would look at me with accusatorial surprise, which made us both laugh.

I took a plastic baggie and pulled the lever down of the malt ball dispenser. Mahogany chocolates nearly the size of golf balls flooded the bag. I tied it with a metal paper tie and wrote down the number of the dispenser. The malt balls were dangerously addicting and apparently potent in calories. I largely attribute the 10 pounds of weight I gained by sophomore year to them. Salvie also grabbed a box of Sour Patch Kids or a bag of gummy worms to complete our movie snacks.

Because of my obsessive fears of weight gain at that time, I tried to work out with Salvie when I visited him as well. Salvie encouraged working out before the movie night. At the UCSD sports area, there was a tractor tire about 1.5 meters high that could be pushed around the track as a resistance exercise. Salvie would pick it up for me, since it was too heavy for me to initially get off the ground, and then I pushed it around the track while he did pull ups at the bars nearby. Salvie could do a lot of pulls ups. But he too started to pack on some extra insulation from the malt balls. I slacked and did not push myself too hard. In an accurate rendition of

Arnold Schwarzenegger's voice from the movie *Kindergarten Cop,* Salvie would tease, *"you lack discipline."* Arnold Schwarzenegger says this line to an unruly class of kindergarteners. He is posing undercover as their "teacher" while really trying to catch a drug lord. In the end, Schwarzenegger also humorously achieves an orderly, matured class.

When I wanted to skip working out and go straight to relaxing and watching a movie instead, Salvie would say, "That's your chub talking." It was true. My chub wanted malt balls and ease, no suffering from working out. I did lack discipline.

Salvie sometimes picked me up from my school to take me for a drive. When I was a freshman, I lived in the women's dorms of the University of San Diego, south of his school. Salvie had a 1990 Ford Ranger that he inherited from our uncle. He had raised and altered it, which gave it a distinctive growl.

I looked out from my second-floor window. Past the palm fronds and onto the street which was flooded with light from the full moon. On that particular Friday night, I was feeling lonely and had called Salvie to chat. Without me asking, he did not hesitate to come and spend his Friday night with me. I heard his truck coming before I could see it, until it roared outside of my dorm. I fled down the wooden stairs and ran across the grass. At 19 and 17 years of age, Salvie and I became better friends than when we were children, bonding over living away from home for the first time and becoming adults in what I believed to be the most beautiful, big city in the world. I slammed the metal door and Salvie started driving. We didn't have a destination in mind that night. Sometimes not knowing where we were going was part of the adventure.

Classic rock from Guns N' Roses, Journey, and Boston filled the cabin and poured out the windows into the night sky. Usually on our drives, Salvie was talkative, and I loved to listen. I would say from the passenger's seat, "Salvie, tell me about the world." And that's all it took for him to begin telling me about current events and his latest theories, ideas, and insights. It felt like hearing my favorite podcast – learning, being entertained, and never wanting it to end. But that night we had less to say. As we looked at the streets of San Diego, I sensed something I couldn't understand, and it felt like aching.

Salvie drove us into Point Loma, a peninsula near downtown San Diego. We reached the other side, a cliff overlooking the Pacific Ocean. The truck settled next to a few other parked cars and quieted. Through the windshield a live theater began – the black, velvety sky was the backdrop, the ocean was an onyx stage, and majestic sapphire clouds hung carefully in their places above us. The full moon, the brilliant main character, was up close and gigantic. We had front row seats. From our car to the moon was a direct path of light on the ocean, like a glistening street of gold. It produced a yearning to run towards it, as if the ocean's surface was a solid glass. But we sat there looking wondrously instead, human eyes determining how it might be possible to contain the endless beauty. The moon was too large, the ocean was too deep. I would never again see that scene exactly as it was that night. The realization that I couldn't keep it all felt strangely painful. A sudden feeling of emptiness crept its way in and gnawed inside of me.

"Knights of Cydonia," by Muse was playing next through the truck speakers as we continued to stare in awe at the heartbreaking view. The last line of the chorus repeated in the air as if it was speaking directly to us and about us, the part where the band sings about how we must fight to survive. I could feel so keenly in that moment the loneliness and disconnection in the city and inside of me, but I felt the words most strongly about Salvie. It felt like our souls and spirits were fighting to survive in surroundings of futility and vanity, a world of meaningless impermanence that failed to be convincing. And it seemed that the most honest thing to do about it was to feel sad. I'm not sure what Salvie was thinking, but I could feel his sadness.

The route back home was going to be straightforward, back down the hills of Point Loma and onto the mainland. About 5 minutes into our drive back, however, we peaked up over a hill that I haven't been able to relocate since. It didn't seem that there could be anything that would match what we had just seen, but a new wonder presented itself. Salvie and I leaned forward with gasps as I motioned excitedly for him to pull over, which he was already doing. To our surprise, in front of us was a 180-degree view of the entire San Diego skyline. The downtown and bay sparkled and glittered from end to end in vivid colors like the Northern lights. On the black, blue water of the bay was an upside-down copy of the same image above it. Both water and sky, all shimmering lights. We happened upon magic twice that night.

After Salvie died, our little sister Maria, who was then 12 years old, had a continuation of the dream I had before he died, the one about the abandoned apartment complex in ruins. I had not told her anything about my dream. In her dream, the parking garage of the Trieste apartments, the apartment that Salvie and I shared during his final year of university, was underwater. The complex was abandoned and covered in vines just as it was in my dream. Maria was swimming in the water towards the level that corresponded with our apartment floor. Perhaps the moving gray clouds in my dream had later produced the rain that flooded her dream – maybe water I had been looking for. The water ended like a shoreline at the place where Salvie and I used to park our cars. There, Maria walked the remaining distance from the water's edge to the dry ground of our parking spots. Her dream ended there.

The parking lot was the last place that Maria saw Salvie. My mom had brought her to visit us, and they were heading back home. Salvie and I had walked them out to say goodbye. Maria hugged Salvie once. After he turned, she later said that she felt uneasy and that they shouldn't go. This compelled her to hug him again.

CHARLIE GARDNER

Dr Charlie Gardner is a conservation scientist, environmental activist, and public commentator on climate change, the destruction of nature, and society's responses to them. He is widely quoted on the environment and activism in broadcast, print and online media, and tweets from @CharlieJGardner.

cjamgardner@yahoo.co.uk

I'd Rather be at Work

Glasgow, on a cold November morning, and the world's leaders are meeting at COP26 to discuss taking action on climate change. A mile or so up the River Clyde, where the rain lashes across the George V Bridge, I sit in the road blocking traffic, attached to about 20 other scientists by a chain around my neck. To my left shivers Jorge, a medical student from Spain, and on my right Anders, a retired Swedish sociologist, defiantly ignores his creaking body.

We've been here about four hours, the chain is becoming weighty, and the icy metal bites my skin when it sneaks between my scarves. The initial buzz from evading the swarming police to occupy the bridge is starting to wear off, replaced by numbing cold and creeping self-doubt. I have watched as four of my new friends were cut away by a specialist protest removal team and carried to waiting vans, and now it's my turn. A soft-spoken young officer places safety goggles over my eyes, leans my head to one side, and tries to hold my attention as his colleague begins to hack through the chain. But I'm not really listening.

My mind is elsewhere, consumed by a rather incongruent thought: I'd rather be at work.

For much of my career, work has meant research.

Like many, I felt that the first step to addressing environmental problems was to understand them, so I became a scientist. I went to university, again and again, and got myself some fancy letters. I spent years – my happiest years – in the field collecting data. I published dozens of scientific papers, and I helped translate my research into policy briefs for those in a position to use them.

But while I love research, I didn't just do it for fun. I believed that if scientists worked to provide information, our society's leaders would use that information to make wise decisions in the public interest. Evidence, I believed, would empower us to transition our societies to a safer future.

Alas, I was naïve. For governmental decision-making isn't necessarily based on evidence at all, any more than it is driven by a desire to make wise decisions in the public interest. It is based on power and influence.

And nowhere was this more obvious than along the River Clyde, in the thronging negotiating rooms of COP26.

"The science is clear," proclaimed Joe Biden at the opening of the conference, and indeed it has been for a long time. The French physicist Joseph Fourier observed that the composition of the atmosphere could affect the climate back in 1824, and in 1856 the American Eunice Foote demonstrated the particular danger posed by the heat-trapping properties of carbon dioxide. By the 1950s even the oil companies knew about the impacts of burning fossil fuels[1], and in 1988 the United Nations created the Intergovernmental Panel on Climate Change to synthesise the science for policymakers. It has been churning out authoritative – and ever more alarming – reports ever since.

So yes, President Biden, the science is clear.

The science tells us that climate change is driven by our greenhouse gas emissions, and that 82% of those emissions come from burning fossil fuels[2];

The science tells us that climate change is already killing 5 million people a year[3], and will render most of the tropics uninhabitable to human beings by 2070[4];

The science tells us that climate change may deprive the world of living systems as rich and beautiful as coral reefs and tropical rainforests, within decades[5]; The science tells us that climate change threatens human civilisation itself[6];

And the science tells us that the worst of climate change can still be avoided, if we immediately transition away from our deadly addiction to fossil fuels[7].

On the same day as President Biden's speech, Prime Minister Boris Johnson assured us that "we know what the scientists tell us, and we have learned not to ignore them."

He was lying.

If there's one thing that global leaders have managed to do with the near two centuries' worth of accumulated scientific knowledge, it's ignore it. Their wilful disregard is written into the history of international climate negotiations.

Article 20 of the Glasgow Climate Pact – the final text, agreed by all 196 signatory countries, that emerged from COP26 – contained an otherwise unremarkable sentence about the need to accelerate efforts towards "the phasedown of unabated coal power and phase-out of inefficient fossil fuel subsidies[8]." Unremarkable, that is, were it not for the fact that this was the first time coal, or indeed any fossil fuel, had ever been mentioned in a COP text.

In 25 previous years of negotiations, governments had failed even to mention the main problem. Like spending a quarter century on a global response to Covid-19 without discussing viruses, this is nonsensical, perverse, scarcely even believable. But it is not surprising. Not when one considers that the biggest delegation at COP26, comprising over 500 lobbyists, belonged to the fossil fuel industry[9]. Not when one considers that the largest seat at the negotiating table went to those with a vested interest in preventing the change the world so desperately needs.

Of course, the nefarious influence of these fossil fuel interests also reaches far beyond these international negotiations. Within a week of the end of formal talks at COP26, President Biden's administration held the largest sale of oil and gas leases in US history[10]. The UK, self-proclaimed global climate leader, recently announced a new energy policy promoting the opening of new oil fields in the North Sea[11]. In the words of the world's most senior diplomat, UN Secretary General António Guterres, "some government and business leaders are saying one thing, but doing another. Simply put, they are lying[12]."

Faced with a choice between fossil fuels and a liveable future, our governments have chosen oil and gas. In full awareness of the consequences, they have selected the path that will destroy everything. They have chosen genocide.

Ecocide.

Omnicide.

So this is where I find myself, as an Earth scientist in a planetary emergency. My faith that knowledge would ensure a better world has been shattered, and my dream of a career doing interesting research lies in ruins. Climate change means my hopes for a peaceful and prosperous future will never be realised, and my belief that my government is working to keep me safe has been exposed as dangerously deluded.

What else is a scientist to do, when my years of training in critical thinking and evaluation of the evidence lead me to the inescapable conclusion that the system I live in is destroying everything I hold dear? What else is a citizen to do, when the evidence suggests our leaders are committed to such an outcome? If I cannot be a bystander, and will not be complicit, there seems only one option.

Resistance.

I didn't want to block the George V Bridge, that rainy day at COP26. I knew that I would be arrested, and that I'd likely spend a lonely night in a police cell. I knew it might affect my reputation, my career, and even my rights and freedoms. I knew it would be stressful, and that I'd struggle to concentrate or sleep for days beforehand. And I worried it could be traumatic.

But I also knew that nothing else has worked.

Ceaseless campaigning and myriad legal challenges have achieved little, and detailed warnings of our impending doom haven't been enough to persuade our leaders to change course. Knowledge alone is insufficient, because this isn't an information deficit problem. This is a battle of power and influence, and those who have it, those who have grown rich beyond imagining as the beneficiaries of the status quo, have invested heavily in ensuring nothing changes. In a struggle to shape policies that will determine the fate of the world, we scientists came armed merely with graphs and data, while the fossil fuel companies brought billions of dollars and spent it corrupting the democratic process[13] and convincing the public that climate change either wasn't real, or wasn't a problem[14].

If scientists' warnings had fallen on unlistening ears, unheralded by the media and unheeded by politicians and the public, then we would have to communicate more effectively. We would have to become more influential, harder to ignore. And what more powerful way to communicate could there be than putting our bodies on the line? If reports alone had failed, what more could scientists do to break the silence and demonstrate the severity of this crisis, than to provoke a mass arrest[15]?

Nothing makes one question one's decisions like sitting in a police cell, and my time as a guest of Glasgow's finest, that wet November evening, was difficult and uncomfortable. Hunched on a blue plastic mattress, tracing patterns in a tray of grey baked beans with a cardboard spork, my thoughts were interrupted only by the violent, hourly opening of the door hatch as an officer checked on my welfare. Physically I was fine – I'd been able to change into a regulation grey tracksuit and they'd given me an extra blanket – but I was otherwise ill at ease. I had spent years training for a professional career, but just as I should have been settling down to a life of rewarding research, I had chosen to jeopardise it all. At times I persuaded myself that I was foolish, perhaps even mad. Yet one word, swirling and contorting around my mind, kept reminding me of my sanity.

Emergency.

Of course I would rather be at work than fomenting an uprising. But this is a planetary emergency and, in an emergency, we take urgent action.

In a planetary emergency, resistance is the work now.

---

1. See e.g. Watts, J. et al. (2019) Half a century of dither and denial – a climate crisis timeline. *The Guardian*, 9th October 2019.
2. This refers specifically to emissions in 1957–2017. Le Quéré, C. et al. (2018) Global Carbon Budget 2018. *Earth System Science Data* 10: 2141–2194.
3. Lombrana, L.M. (2021) Climate change linked to 5 million deaths a year, new study shows. *Bloomberg*, 7th July 2021.
4. Xu, C. et al. (2020) Future of the human climate niche. *Proceedings of the National Academy of Sciences USA* 117: 11350–11355.
5. For coral reefs, see Hoegh-Guldberg, O. et al. (2017) Coral reef ecosystems under climate change and ocean acidification. *Frontiers in Marine Science* 4: 158. For forests, see e.g. Brodribb, T.J. et al. (2020) Hanging by a thread? Forests and drought. *Science* 368: 261–266, and Trisos, C. et al. (2021) The projected timing of abrupt ecological disruption from climate change. *Nature* 580: 496–501.
6. All human civilisations developed during the last 12,000 years, a period of remarkable climatic stability called the Holocene. Climatic stability is required for agriculture, which provides the food surpluses that allow for the division of labour and organised society. We have now left the stability of the Holocene, and climate-driven 'simultaneous breadbasket failure' is the most likely driver of societal collapse. See e.g. Servigne, P. & Stevens, R. *How Everything Can Collapse* (Polity, 2020).
7. IPCC. *Climate Change 2022: Mitigation of Climate Change. Summary for Policymakers* (Intergovernmental Panel on Climate Change, 2022).
8. UNFCCC Decision -/CP.26 Glasgow Climate Pact. Available at https://unfccc.int/documents/310475.
9. McGrath, M. (2021) COP26: Fossil fuel industry has largest delegation at climate summit. *BBC News*, 8th November 2021.
10. Noor, D. (2021) Biden administration holds largest oil and gas sale in US history. *Boston Globe*, 17th November 2021.
11. Gardner, C. et al. (2022) Extinction Rebellion scientists: why we glued ourselves to a government department. *The Conversation*, 26th April 2022.
12. António Guterres video message on launch of IPCC Working Group 3 report on mitigation, 4th April 2022.
13. In 2020, for example, oil and gas companies spent $136 million on political contributions and $110 million on lobbying in the USA. That's a quarter of a billion dollars in just one country, in just one year, and just one corporate sector (OpenSecrets.org).
14. Fossil fuel interests have orchestrated a massive, ongoing disinformation campaign since the 1980s. See e.g. Supran, G. & Oreskes, N. (2021) The forgotten oil ads that told us climate change was nothing. *The Guardian*, 18th November 2021.
15. The Scientist Rebellion bridge block at COP26 resulted in 21 arrests, of which 18 scientists, see Thompson, T. (2021) Scientist Rebellion: researchers join protesters at COP26. *Nature* 599: 357.

EDWARD GRIERSON

Edward Grierson began writing by keeping a nature blog. This led to him contributing to blogs such as *Common by Nature*, and publications such as *New Nature, The Norwich Radical,* and *Concrete.* He now seeks to make his writing less matter of fact, more ambiguous, and more open to interpretation.

Ejgrier1998@gmail.com

Crocodiles

When I was a child, any holiday or day out required a trip to the local zoo. And no such trip was complete until I had been through the reptile house. Edinburgh, my nearest zoo, really understood this. The site is situated on the slope of Costrophine Hill, with the main pathway being a climb to the top, and the position of its reptile house made it one of the last exhibits on a visit. This gave it a sense of finality – the rest of the day was all a build-up to the reptile house.

Nowadays, these buildings are considered outdated. Like VHS tapes, cathode ray TVs, and analogue cameras, buildings specifically for cold-blooded creatures were at the end of their existence when I was growing up. As the new millennium progressed, zoos placed increasing emphasis on immersion; reptiles were moved out of their self-contained spaces, and integrated into exhibits that recreate the mangroves of Bangladesh, the Pantanal, or the Tsavo plains. Many excel in this. But in my opinion, they simply can't replicate the experience of entering a reptile house, and feeling as if you have entered another world altogether.

Edinburgh Zoo's reptile house managed this perfectly. Once you walked through the heavy wooden doors, you were sealed off from outside. The new world you entered was pitch-dark, except for a strange red light with no identifiable source. There was always a flat hum of insects, the sort you hear in a rainforest at night. The sound of running water, running from unseen streams in unknowable directions. Lining both walls were rows of terraria, whose inhabitants were completely unlike humans. I would pass poison dart frogs, boa constrictors and beaded lizards; they hardly ever moved, but always stared back.

But the centrepiece, the one I always gravitated towards, was the big tank. Somewhere, in what seemed like an endless hemisphere of water, the crocodile was always waiting.

It rarely did much; it didn't need to. Just its presence could spark a sense of unease that penetrated the deepest corners of my mind. This wasn't just a case of a big carnivore that could eat me up. Plenty of other animals at the zoo could do that. The crocodile struck something far deeper.

Maybe it was due to how unnatural it seemed; not just inhuman, but almost non-animal too. Its pointed teeth stuck out in odd places. Its body was composed of jagged edges, all hard and impenetrable. Every part of it, even the joints, composed of interlocking rows of square scales, as if its body was some suit of armour. It was almost mechanical. With flesh-and-blood animals, you felt as if you could at least understand them. With this crocodile, there was no such sense of relatability.

The crocodile's exhibit also provided a lot for the imagination. The other tanks and terraria were starkly illuminated, allowing you to see every detail of the inhabitants. It was the equivalent of yelling "Look!" or "see here!" – a tactic that gets attention, but can become obnoxious after a while, and doesn't allow for any self-discovery. No strobe lights illuminated the crocodile's tank. I couldn't just look at it; I had to peer into its enclosure, through the murky water, to find it. And the gloomy tank never gave away all its secrets; I could never fully make out its inhabitant. Watching the crocodile was a far more subtle viewing experience. It felt earned, rather than thrust at you, it didn't reveal everything, and it allowed you to come to your own conclusions about what you were seeing.

As for the details that I couldn't make out, my mind was able to fill that in. In this process, the crocodile transformed into something far stranger, darker, and unknowable. It was something with no features that I could distinguish, and whose dimensions couldn't possibly be comprehended. In the total darkness of the reptile house, I could imagine this creature lurking in every corner at once.

But despite the fear it inspired in me, I always felt an equally strong sense of fascination. In fact, my fear and my fascination with it were inseparable. It was like watching a horror movie with one eye open. There were other animals that I was afraid of: scorpions, porcupines, gorillas. But whenever I saw these animals at a zoo, I turn the other way. Crocodiles drew me into their world, and no matter how uneasy I felt around them, I never wanted to look away. Seeing it became a form of reverence. Just as many Christians sought to be reminded of Jesus' suffering, I kept visiting this crocodile to remind me of how cruel and deadly my religion- the natural world- could be.

In hindsight, the reptile house at Edinburgh Zoo was very much a product of my imagination. The crocodile was a dwarf species, which looked slightly bigger due to the glass. The building itself was just a black, rectangular box, the architectural equivalent of a rug draped over some sticks.

There was no light, except from the terrariums, and no sound. I can't even remember if the crocodile ever did much in its tank, besides float on the top and lie on the bottom.

But the reality didn't matter. What mattered was its effect in my mind. This crocodile had grafted itself onto my malleable young imagination. It was always with me, always just out of sight in my mind. It almost became a personal mythical creature. And so, a fearful obsession was formed, one that would never be completely shaken off.

—

In sharp contrast to Edinburgh, Dublin Zoo's reptile house left little to be imagined. Built in 1902, this reptile house was a charming Neo-Gothic construction. A ceiling of vaulted arches, cloisonne windows, and a tiled floor. It was always very well-lit, leaving no room for hidden dangers. The atmosphere inside was muggy but sterile, like an office. It was the sort of atmosphere that I would usually have found uncomfortable. But here, it matched the sterile, lethargic lives of its inhabitants. Since it was much better lit, the lethargy of the cold-blooded creatures was more apparent. Nowhere was this made clearer than through their Nile Crocodile.

This size of this creature in my mind was matched by the scale in real life; this was a crocodile that really could have eaten me. Sometimes, crouching down on my knees just in front of the enclosure, I was nose-to-nose with it. All that separated us was a thin wall of glass. It goes without saying that it didn't seem to offer much protection from the seven-foot beast within touching distance.

I visited Dublin Zoo on every trip to Ireland for the first decade of my life, and on every visit to the reptile house, the crocodile always seemed to be in the exact same spot, in the exact same position. Its mouth was always open, always at the same angle, and always with the same leering grin. The only movement I ever saw was the twitching of its cool yellow eyes.

Crocodiles are exceptionally long-lived, to the point that we don't properly know the full extent of their lifespan. Some captive specimens have been recorded at seventy years old, but some of these may have been even older. People simply haven't lived long enough to properly record their age. This specimen could lie in the same position seemingly for years at a time, as if those years were just a few seconds. It proved to me that these animals operated on a different timescale, one in which we are as small to them as our pets are in our life spans.

This was solidified a few years ago, when I revisited Dublin Zoo. In the intervening years, the reptile house had been completely redesigned, into an ultra-modern assemblage of steel, concrete and linoleum flooring. Clearly the designers had noticed how the old building had the air of an office and had decided to one-up it, by giving this new building the look of an office. Inside the building, the dinosaur skeletons and diagrams of Earth's tectonic plates gave away the reason for the redesign: it had been to coincide with the release of *Jurassic World*, due to the obvious, if tangential, connection to reptiles. The new building certainly fitted *Jurassic World*, by being a shallow, unoriginal imitation of its far greater predecessor. But one thing that hadn't changed was the Nile Crocodile. It was in a new tank, made of concrete and mortar and with far more sand and vegetation. But its jaws were still open at the same angle, with the exact same grin.

In a way, Dublin's crocodile felt like a natural progression from Edinburgh's. The little Dwarf crocodile had spawned a creature in my psyche; this crocodile was that creature in the flesh, brought into light.

—

When I was eleven, I saw a Nile Crocodile in the wild. We were in the Serengeti, and had driven to the bank of the Grumeti River. It was a spot where the tourists could get out of their safari vehicles and stretch their legs. We could also observe the hippos that were lying in the river in droves, with only their eyes and ears peeking above the surface. But today, they had company. Lounging on the bank opposite me, no more than thirty yards away, a crocodile sat on the rocks, its mouth open in exactly the same position as the Dublin Zoo individual.

For the first time, when I watched a crocodile, it was with a feeling of anticipation. This specimen was representing crocodiles in their wild state. This time there really was no glass. It could take me there and then. So what did it do, to strike fear and awe into me?

It just lay there. Captivity clearly had no effect on crocodiles' behaviour; in the wild, they are just as unflinching. I'm not sure I even saw this one's eyes move.

A crocodile's world moves at a glacial pace. It's a pace that fits their evolution. Crocodilians evolved at the same time as the first dinosaurs, and over millions of years diversified into dinosaur-sized dinosaur-hunters, hoofed runners, ocean-goers, pig-nosed burrowers, and even flat-faced foragers. The crocodylia – the order that modern crocodiles, alligators, and caimans belong to – first evolved 90 million years ago, and made it through the Mass Extinction at the end of the Cretaceous period. There is a macabre poignancy about their survival: the fact that, in the age of mammals, there are still some reptiles that carry on the dinosaurs' torch, and still present a danger to us. That it can be seen as a danger without having to do anything is a real achievement.

When this is the case, and when time moves so slowly for them, they can afford to wait. Other defenceless animals would pass by the same bank on better days, when the temperature was warmer, or the river had less hippos. It could afford to let me go, leaving me with nothing but an image of a ten-foot, wild Nile crocodile, an image that was already transforming inside my head, into something far stranger.

SARA KATSCHKA

Sara Katschka was born and raised in Ohio, USA. She studied English literature and creative writing, and French at the University of Iowa. After finishing her degree, she spent two years teaching English in France. Since then, she has also worked as a bookseller and a long-term substitute teacher.

sarakatschka@yahoo.com

They're Coming
An extract from a longer essay.

I sit on my bed, duvet tucked around my knees. There is a wine glass full of cider cradled in the palms of my hands. The cider carries notes of the Prosecco that came before it. I scratch my nails against the smooth glass surface. Scratch at the tightly wound knots inside of me. I must loosen them before they crack a rib.

I search for a movie or show to keep the alcohol company.

A glimpse of a particular thumbnail makes me pause, scroll back up. The image is of a blonde woman in a white tank top. Blood is smeared along her jawline, across both her shoulders and the material of her shirt. She stands in front of an open car door, looking at something out of frame. I know this woman, and exactly what she's looking at.

It is the 2004 remake of George A. Romero's *Dawn of the Dead*.

I feel that familiar pull.

It will be fine. I haven't seen it in over fourteen years. I know the entire plot. There are no surprises. And I've been drinking. It will be fine.

Hitting play is like hitting a self-destruct button.

———

Immediately after I turned eleven and finished elementary school, my family moved from our small two-story brick home to a larger, newer one on the other side of town. There was so much space in that house in comparison to the old one. The living room was wide and open, with thick beige carpeting which was soft beneath my feet. Perfect for dancing on. The second floor had a balcony that looked down on the living room. We now had a *basement*. And a *garage*. The picture of suburbia.

The main difference in living in this house was that instead of walking home from school every day, I took the bus. My older brother, now starting high school, preferred to walk the three miles home from his high school rather than take the bus.

"Why waste all that time walking home?" I asked him after the first or second week of the school year.

"You're in middle school now. You'll see for yourself soon enough."

I knew that middle school had been difficult for my brother, but I was convinced that my experience would be different than his. His insistence on walking meant that I was home alone for an hour or sometimes more. I'd been home alone before, but never this consistently.

It was on one of these afternoons that I watched my first horror movie: *Dawn of the Dead*. There were only twenty minutes left when I turned it on. I sat there on the couch and watched the end play out. The main group of survivors had just left the mall where they had been holding out. Now they were making their way towards Lake Michigan, where they hoped to take a boat to a small island with supposedly few inhabitants. That's where everything went wrong.

In the span of a few minutes, the number of survivors dwindled from nine to five. Then, at the last minute, one of the leading male characters revealed that he had been bitten and therefore could not go with them to the island. A blonde woman, Anna, protested. But she also knew that it was too late for him. The movie ended with four survivors on the boat, the last one watching them sail away. As the screen faded to black, there was a gunshot.

I stared at the credits, unsure of what I felt. My heart was pounding. I pressed my hand against my chest, felt my heart jump up to meet my hand. Was I scared? Was I excited? I didn't know.

Before that, my primary experience with horror movies came from my family's bi-weekly trip to Blockbuster Video. While my parents stood shoulder to shoulder and discussed which movies to rent, I wandered through the aisles, picking up DVD cases here and there. I squinted at the cover art, before twisting the case around to read the summaries on the back. Often, I found myself drawn to the horror section. Compared to the films we normally rented, films like *Sky High* or *The Princess Diaries 2: Royal Engagement*, these covers were much darker. They were black, gray, dark green. When brighter colors like orange, white, or red were used on them, it only made the cover look that much more sinister. And to grasp what was happening on the cover, I often had to look closely. I avoided slasher films and looked for the more supernatural ones. Vampires, ghosts, werewolves, demons, zombies. That was what I was after. Something that could stimulate my imagination for hours afterwards. Throughout all my surveying, I noticed that bad things always seemed to be happening to teenagers. Like with my brother, I should've understood the warning signs.

I didn't know whether I liked what I had seen in *Dawn of the Dead*. I only knew that I felt a certain thrill at finally seeing a horror movie, of having accessed it on my own.

That movie always seemed to be on TV when I got home from school. I kept turning on and watching it. Watching it in pieces. Ten minutes in the middle. The first half hour. The entire second half. I watched it until I had completed the whole puzzle.

I began to notice how quiet the house was. A quiet that existed beneath the constant hum of the fridge, the passing of cars and sputtering school buses on the way to the elementary school behind my house, the high-pitched shrieks of the next-door neighbors splashing around in their pool. I went around the house making as much noise as possible. Slamming my backpack down on the green tiles of the entryway. Pressing down on the keys of my mom's out of tune piano on my way to the kitchen. I would eventually resume my usual position on the couch, turning the volume of *Dawn of The Dead* all the way up until I heard the family knock. *Duh duh duhduh duh   duh duh.*

I'm not sure when the dreams began. Suddenly I was unable to dream of anything else but the beginning of the movie. The way Anna's bedroom door, already halfway open, slowly swings open to reveal a blonde girl standing there in a long, pink nightgown. The way she steps into the light, and you see that something is very wrong.

I dreamt of my own door slowly opening. Sometimes there would be nothing there but bloody footprints on the beige carpet. Other times she would simply stand there. I'd stare at the part of her cheek that was missing, the exposed teeth, stained red. Drool dripped from her chin.

Other times she rushed forward as she did on screen. I dreamt of her teeth, startling sharp, ripping into my neck, pulling at the muscle. The way it would stretch and tear as I backed up, comically long like some handkerchief pulled from a magician's sleeve.

Once I even dreamt that I was standing at the door of my parents' bedroom, hungry.

The nightmares released me into the early hours of the morning. Disoriented, I anchored my fingers to the warm, scratchy sheets beneath me and tried to remain as still as possible. *Don'tmove. Don'tlook. Don'tspeak. Don'tmove don'tlook-*I listened for movement outside. Downstairs. The sound of her breath, of her snarls, a constant ringing in my ear. It took me hours to get back to sleep.

Even when I stopped watching the movie altogether the dreams didn't stop.

I began to lock my door at night. No zombie could get me if my door was locked. Or at least I would know if it was there. I figured that I was not the type to last long in a zombie apocalypse, but the worst thing I could think of was being caught unaware of what was happening. What was coming.

I'd never been afraid of the dark, but I started to leave my lights on at night. That wasn't enough. I still wouldn't be able to see any zombie approach the door. I needed to leave the bathroom light on as well. Although my parents reminded me every so often of what that did to the energy bill, they left the light on in periods where the dreams were particularly bad.

I counted down a year and a half to the 2008 election. It had a hidden special meaning to me. Different from the meaning for the rest of the nation. In the title sequence of *Dawn of the Dead*, I remembered, incorrectly in the end, that there was a shot of a zombified George W Bush. Once the election happened and George W. Bush was replaced, then the events of that movie could no longer happen.

The passing of the election did help. I was out of immediate danger. As I started high school and joined marching band, I experienced a gradual return to the land of the living. The dreams became more infrequent, enough to slightly let my guard down. But they didn't disappear completely. Their reappearances became almost a running joke with my parents.

"Did you sleep alright?" My mom would ask.

"Oh, I had another zombie dream" I'd reply casually, lips pressed to the rim of my cereal bowl to catch the last drops of milk.

I slept with my door locked and my light on until I left for college.

—

A quarter of the way into the movie and I find that I cannot look directly at the screen. Nothing bad is happening now, but I know that isn't going to be the case for long. A few of the survivors, who the main characters have just let into the mall, are going to turn. I try drinking more and looking at it through the amber filter of my wine glass. *My housemates are here. I am safe. Nothing is going to happen.*

I feel a tingling sensation in my arms that is not normal. I fidget to try to shake off the feeling. In my chest my heart is palpitating. And everything in me focuses on that feeling. I lean back against the radiator.

I'm

goingto

faint.

What if what I'm feeling is not the precursor to fainting, but to dying? *Ican'tdothis.*

I push my laptop down the bed and get to my feet, shove my head out my bedroom window, gulp in the biting wind. A drop of sweat falls into my eye.

I quickly put on *Shaun of the Dead* to prove that I can handle zombies. *See? They're not a big deal.* Even now I find myself constantly skipping fifteen seconds ahead. I finish the movie in under half of its actual run time.

JENNIFER KNIGHTS

Jennifer Knights is a former criminal lawyer living in north Norfolk. She has a fascination with why individuals spin stories and persist with their untruths in the face of all reason. Jennifer is currently researching the life of a complex local character. She aims to write non-fiction both about his truths and his apparently blatant inventions.

jennyknights23@gmail.com

An Interview – Burgh-next-Aylsham, Norfolk
March 1976

Marcus La Touche sprang from his tiny mould-spattered caravan. The sixty-five-year-old sported a conical hat and a clown costume quartered in shades of ruby and gold. His disconcerted visitor noticed the older man wore incongruous brown brogues. Perhaps swollen-toed clown shoes were impossible to manage on wet grass.

The clown laughed, his mouth mimicking the crimson grin painted far beyond his lip line and extending towards his cheekbones. Leichner white clogged his goatee beard and his kohl-lined eyes creased with merriment. 'Bruce! How good of you to come old chap!' The clown pulled gently at the side seams of his baggy three quarter length trousers and curtseyed a greeting. 'I thought I should wear this. You'll want to photograph me dressed as Clown Roma, won't you.'

A lurcher dog barked and jumped up at the stranger. 'Boby, down!' the elderly entertainer bellowed. 'Allow me to introduce Boby Hooligan.' The dog raised one paw in greeting. Bruce was about to stroke the animal when his host announced 'Come! Let us inspect my latest groundworks.'

Bruce Robinson, a well-respected sports journalist at the Eastern Daily Press, had received an anonymous letter telling him that he would find a semi-retired clown living beside the River Bure. It is highly likely that Marcus wrote the letter himself, seeking to boost his moribund career. Sometimes Marcus deployed his alter ego, 'Arthur Aston, Promoter and Agent' to publicise performances. Even in the most difficult of circumstances Marcus was adept at courting the press.

His first caravan was destroyed by fire near Skegness Winter Gardens on 21st July 1948. Later that same day he told the *Skegness Standard* that only his sixteen-year-old 'talking dog' Viscount and Boy, Viscount's understudy, were rescued from the inferno. Despite losing his home, his possessions and £20 in cash, Marcus was sufficiently composed to give a full resumé of the older dog's achievements calling him 'a star of stage, screen and radio'. The paper reported that Viscount had featured on TV twice, broadcast on the radio on thirteen occasions and 'starred' in seventeen films. The dog's war record was also related in detail. Trained to carry messages for the Local Defence Volunteers Viscount had endured five blitzes.

Another of Marcus' promotional ploys was to replicate a Hollywood stunt first utilised in the 1940s when Twentieth Century-Fox reputedly insured Betty Grable's legs for $1million. In 1961 Marcus managed to convince both the *Daily Express* and the *Daily Mail* that his new dog Bingo, another canine genius, was the subject of a £10,000 insurance policy 'against loss of bark'. Subsequent articles extolled the dog's mathematical ability and made it clear that Bingo – along with his master – was keen to visit schools to help children with their arithmetic. The columns were syndicated worldwide, but little work came of it.

Before his visit in the spring of 1976, the EDP journalist would have understood the motivation for the anonymous letter. Most likely he was expecting to discuss Marcus's appearances at charity fetes and his availability for children's parties. Instead, he found himself inspecting a drainage channel with Clown Roma in full fig.

The River Bure has always flooded – the landscape is flat with little fall in the ground level between Burgh and the coast. The river water meanders through the Broads at Wroxham and on to the North Sea at Breydon Water. In autumn the water meadows flood and can freeze in winter. Marooned on the riverbank for several months the nine by five-foot caravan was now immovable. Marcus needed to divert some of the water should there be another autumn deluge. He claimed to have dug a two-hundred-yard channel by hand in the space of fourteen days.

Wandering along the journalist nodded towards the new ditch. 'Was it difficult?'[1]

'Yes, but I turned it into a game,' Marcus replied. 'If you do that hard work becomes enjoyable.' His tone was high and clipped, a voice from a bygone era of BBC English and Received Pronunciation.[2] 'In 1962 I became a clown. Since then everything has been very wonderful for me.'

Bruce raised an eyebrow – the situation did not look particularly wonderful. Sensing his visitor's scepticism, the clown continued, 'I have my pipe, I have food. I have the most wonderful plays and music on the radio, and I have four amazing works of art. Come and see them, do.'

Returning to the caravan Marcus gestured to the algae-smeared windows. 'You see, dear boy, I have marvellous ever-changing views.' Semaphoring

---

[1] This stilted conversation is from the EDP news article 'The Simple Life of a Happy Man' dated 15.3.1976.
[2] Marcus's voice is audible on Pathe newsreels.

his arms in each direction he continued, 'The river, the meadows, the trees and flowers, the sky and birds.' As if on cue a heron hoist itself into the air from amongst the reed beds and made its ungainly way downstream.

'Cup of tea, old chap?'

As Marcus bustled around boiling a kettle on the paraffin stove, Bruce glimpsed inside the grubby caravan. His gaze took in a narrow bunk, a crumpled dog blanket beneath. There was scant room for clothes or other personal possessions. He forbore to ask where Mr La Touche might wash or relieve himself. Perhaps the neighbours at Bridge Cottage gave him access to their outside privy. Yet despite the hardships that must have arisen living in a ramshackle caravan, the clown really did seem remarkably content.

Bruce gazed at the older man's bony back and jutting shoulders. Good job Marcus was entitled to the old age pension. It was probably the steadiest income that his interviewee had received in years.

A fixed address was needed to secure regular payments. Maybe that was the reason why Marcus decided settle in Burgh. The clown had charm and good manners and his bohemian lifestyle became accepted in the village. Housewives kind enough to bring Marcus a casserole or a few eggs sometimes found a bouquet of wildflowers left on the doorstep by way of thanks. In becoming a well-known local character he was able to cadge lifts and rarely had to walk both to and from Aylsham to collect provisions.

Two miles distant the market town provided facilities the village could not. The Post Office supplied an ever-changing audience as he queued to collect his weekly pittance. Bruce could easily imagine Marcus sweeping theatrically into the newsagents, purchasing a tin of St Bruno and his copy of the *Stage* before informing the staff and waiting customers that he was still resting, awaiting a call from his agent.

Inside the caravan the kettle whistled loudly. Marcus crashed around making tea, chattering to his dog. 'Boby, in a moment we will show our visitor how well you can count... do try to concentrate.'

Boby could be heard barking enthusiastically. 'No Boby. Wait!'

Sweeping out of the caravan Marcus thrust two cups and saucers towards Bruce with a flourish. He made great play of opening a deckchair wrongly, doing a bit of clown business, flipping the thin frame this way and that before finally setting it down. Placing a dining chair beside a dilapidated picket fence, Marcus sat at a precarious angle. As the thin wooden legs sank in the mud he laughed and suggested that this was a good place to take a photograph or two.

After the shots were taken Marcus gestured for Bruce to sit in the mildewed canvas deckchair. 'Dear boy, do take a pew – it's quite safe.'

The fabric sling creaked alarmingly as Bruce lowered himself into it. Marcus smiled, his huge, disturbing clown smile, 'Before we start the interview Boby would like to show you how clever he is.' Trapped in a decrepit deckchair it was impossible to avoid the demonstration.

'Boby, what is two add three?'

Boby barked five times, stopped and wagged his tail. Marcus did not appear to have blinked nor moved a finger.

'Can I try?'

'By all means, dear chap.'

'Boby, what is four subtract one?'

Boby held his head to one side looking quizzical. Marcus repeated the question. Boby barked three times. Bruce could not detect a flicker of movement from the dog's owner. After witnessing further examples of addition and subtraction Bruce admitted defeat.

'You're good, you are... both of you.'

'Why thank you, we've had years of practice. Sadly, Boby can only count to twenty. My first dog, Viscount, could count to one hundred ... marvellous dog he was, simply marvellous...'

Although it is not mentioned in the newspaper article, it is highly likely that Boby was told to 'Stand' and promptly sat down or remained on all fours on hearing the command 'Sit!' Each and every one of Marcus's performing dogs learnt this trick. All of them could answer simple questions with one bark for 'yes' and two for 'no' with no visible hint of how their owner was directing them.

The interview lasted for hours. Bruce covered page after page in his spiral notebook with shorthand as Marcus sucked on his briarwood pipe and rehashed his oft-repeated stories. Tales of Huguenot antecedents and his mother's acting career led on to his great-grandfather's fifty-eight-year stint as organist at Norwich Cathedral and the story of his aunt, the author of the longest poem in the English language. However improbable these anecdotes may seem, all are verifiably true – the poem runs to eight volumes.

Marcus' other recollections are harder to pin down. He said his mother found him a role in silent movies before he was five. He claimed to have absconded from boarding school and joined the circus at the age of thirteen and a half. And if that is so, his fiancée, a trapeze artiste, could have plunged to her death at his feet. He may even have suffered a broken back when a lightning strike snapped the king pole in the Big Top. Perhaps he sailed to South America to recuperate, but there are no traces of him on any ship's manifest.

Since it is true he trained animals in Shepperton Studios, it is tempting to believe his tales of work in Hollywood. While there he could well have befriended and played cricket with movie stars and subsequently travelled to Africa on safari with a film crew. On his return to Britain there is nothing to disprove that he performed in front of Winston Churchill and members of the Royal Family.

Bruce Robinson was used to recording facts, the goals, the fouls, the joy and despair of football fans at Carrow Road. By contrast Marcus' stories were unfocussed and extravagant - a *Boys' Own* collage of adventures. Marcus was unable to verify his claims.

'I had newspaper cuttings. Dozens of them. But there was a fire, in Baldock, in my caravan. My dogs Goldie and Viscount II died. I lost everything...'

Another conflagration. Marcus did not tell Bruce of the earlier blaze in Skegness.

As dusk fell the men parted, Marcus still laughing in the fading light.

When *The Simple Life of a Happy Man* was published Bruce Robinson carefully avoided commenting on the veracity of the stories. He remained in contact with Marcus La Touche for a while. They lunched at Jarrolds in Norwich, Marcus arriving in another costume – the attire of a country gentleman – Norfolk jacket, deerstalker and of course sensible brown brogues.

Bruce remained beguiled by the intriguing man he had met on the riverbank. Almost forty years later he blogged about his further investigations into Marcus' stories, still unable to ascertain where the truth lay.

It is undeniable that Marcus craved recognition. Before his death he created a fresh trail of clues, donating his clown costume, doghair encrusted socks and papers to Norwich Castle Museum. The documents include beginnings of an autobiography – ending in his seventh year – and a fuller biography of Viscount, his first performing dog.

A note in Marcus' hand asks, 'Is Clown Roma telling the truth? Well, my friend you are the judge.'

HANNAH MURGATROYD

Hannah Murgatroyd became disabled at the age of 15 and soon began to experience the discrimination that disabled people face, both on a social and an institutional level. Since this, she has fought to ensure that disabled people get the help and support they need, along with protesting against injustices wrought on them by the government.

hgmurgatroyd@gmail.com

Disabled Dread

The dreaded brown envelope is known to many disabled people in the UK. It sits on your doormat or in your letterbox taunting you as you stare in horror at your misfortune. Occasionally, it brings good news. You, or your carer, open the envelope with trembling hands, cursing the Department for Work and Pensions, only to see a small, simple letter.

'We are writing to inform you that you will be receiving a £10 Christmas bonus.'[1]

Both relief and frustration flood through you at once as you exhale a lungful of air and throw the letter away. I'm grateful for this £10 Christmas bonus, even if it'll only buy me a set of Christmas crackers or a couple packs of pigs in blankets. It certainly won't pay for a new set of wheelchair tyres. No matter, it's better than nothing. It's the audacity of sending good news in a brown envelope which leaves me seething. Don't they know the trauma they've inflicted on disabled people with these envelopes?

Then there's the brown envelopes that bring heart stopping news, the ones which can ruin your life and make you homeless.

'We are writing to inform you that your Employment and Support Allowance has been suspended from the 1st of January 2020'[2] on a letter dated the 4th of January. Some forewarning would be nice, but they don't grant you that. Even though the miscalculation of your benefits was entirely their fault.

I've had more bad news envelopes than good news envelopes. Particularly the ones that declare:

'I have looked at your PIP and decided:
- *I can still award you the standard rate of £55.65 a week to help with your daily living needs. You can now get this from 4 July 2017 to 26 June 2021*
- *I can award you the standard rate of £22.00 a week to help with your mobility needs. You can now get this from 4 July 2017 to 26 June 2021'.*[3]

It is this which makes the brown envelopes so traumatic and so upsetting

---

1 Not the actual wording of the letter as this was quoted from memory.
2 Actual wording of the letter I received.
3 Actual wording of a copy of the letter I received.

for me. Getting this through the post crushes you. Personal Independence Payment is a non-means tested disability benefit. It was designed to replace Daily Living Allowance and is a nightmare to apply for. But it's also essential. Without that money I'd have no way of keeping my wheelchair in working order. This benefit is how many disabled people have a car which suits their needs. It's a necessity. When I received this letter, I had previously been receiving the standard rate of daily living and the enhanced rate for mobility needs. I was livid with this decision to reduce my mobility allowance and I went through the rest of the letter, wanting to know why they'd deducted my mobility. How they'd decided that I'd magically been cured.

And it was right there, in plain writing. '*You were able to stand unaided for a short period of time approximately 3 minutes before the pain became too much. I have therefore decided you can stand and then move using an aid or appliance more than 20 meters but not more than 50 meters.*' [4]

I fumed as I read this letter. I hadn't stood for three minutes during my assessment. I'd stood, taken two shaky steps with my crutches, and then sat down. In addition, standing for three minutes does not demonstrate an ability to walk over 20 meters. Standing is so much different than walking. Personally, standing gives me the balance of two feet while leaning heavily on my crutches. Walking involves me swinging both legs together, putting pressure on my shoulders and back. It is excruciating and dangerous. I have fallen and caused permanent damage to my hip by using crutches. This was nonsense, pure nonsense. PIP has rules. They're supposed to demonstrate that, to get the standard rate of mobility, you can walk over 20 meters safely, repeatedly, reliably and in good time.[5] I knew this from my previous tribunal.

The previous tribunal where I'd gone to contest the decision to only award me the standard rate for mobility. I'd won that tribunal. And yet here I was again, heading down the same path as before.

It was that memory which made me curse as I opened my letterbox on the 14th of January 2021 and saw the thick, brown envelope. I knew it was coming. I'd been the one to call them to request this form. I had six months until my award for PIP ended, not being on the list for renewal because I won my PIP award at the non-existent tribunal they'd forced me to. Renewal is simple: A small form where you simply state that nothing has changed and send it off.

4 Actual wording of the decision letter I received.
5 "Reliably", *pipinfo*. rightsnet, n.d. https://pipinfo.net/issues/reliably#issues. (accessed 19/05/2021)

I had to reapply. From the beginning. I had to fill out the 33-page[6] form all over again. For the fourth time in six years.

I got to work straight away. I grabbed snacks and a mocha, before going to my desk and opening a Word document. This form is gruelling. It's cruel. It reduces you to nothing but your disability. You can only list the things you can't do.

I skipped the first couple of questions which were on diagnoses and medication/treatments. Those would be easy to fill in, they didn't require much emotional resilience. They're ones I can do once I've reached the full depth of my depression and self-hatred which this form leads me to, like a sailor to siren song.

I start on question 3c, questions a and b just being simple tick boxes that I can do by hand.

'Extra Information – Preparing Food'

'Preparing and cooking food'.[7] It then gives several bullet-pointed prompts. These are important to read and understand fully, as they give you a glimpse into the wording you need to use to be successful in completing this form. There is a right and a wrong way to fill the form in, specific phrases you should use.

For example, if you cannot cook a simple meal using a conventional cooker but can using a microwave, you are awarded two points out of a possible eight for this section. To me, a simple meal is a ready meal being placed in a microwave or tinned soup. So, not knowing any better, I would likely state that I could cook a simple meal in the microwave.

But that's not what the DWP defines as a simple meal.

A simple meal is defined as 'a cooked one-course meal for one using fresh ingredients' and cook is defined as 'heating food at or above waist height'. Therefore, I need assistance to cook a simple meal – assistance being defined as physical intervention by another person. This awards me four points, half of what I need to get the standard rate of daily living and a third of what I need to get the enhanced rate of daily living.[8]

They don't tell you any of this. All this information you have to find out

---

6 "Claiming Personal Independence Payment (PIP) - Fill in the PIP Form", *Turn2us*. n.d. www.turn2us.org.uk/Benefit-guides/Claiming-Personal-Independence-Payment/Fill-in-PIP-form. (accessed 19/05/2021)

7 "PIP2 How Your Disability Affects You Form" *Department for Work and Pensions. n.d.* https://assets.publishing.service.gov.uk/government/uploads/system/uploads/attachment_data/file/713118/pip2-how-your-disability-affects-you-form.pdf (accessed 19/05/2021), p.7

8 "Daily Living – Activity 1: Preparing Food", *PIPInfo*. n.d. https://pipinfo.net/activities/preparing-food. (accessed 19/05/2021)

for yourself.

I sigh heavily and start typing.

'Q3c. *Due to Ehlers-Danlos Syndrome, I have weak fingers and wrists, which are often also painful. I frequently dislocate finger joints and I have unstable wrists which are prone to dislocating. This can happen doing mundane tasks such as writing and putting a shirt on, but also more complex tasks. I first started noticing issues with cooking when I was doing a GCSE in food tech. I took double the time the other students did.*'

"Hannah, stop," I say out loud to my empty room. "What are you doing?"[9]

There's no way I can reference a time in which I could once do this task, a time where I was able to cook well enough to get an A in GCSE food technology. Referencing this would be detrimental. I would, absolutely, lose all hope of scoring points on this section. They need to know what I can't do now, not what I could do seven years ago. They don't care that I used to love baking and found it a comforting outlet. They don't care about my accomplishments.

I am nothing but a lowly cripple.

So instead, I talk about how I can't chop vegetables. That I cannot make myself a simple salad. That I'm unable to cook on the hob, that cooking using the oven risks me falling out of my wheelchair and onto the scalding oven door. That I rely on ready meals and takeout, even though this is detrimental to my diabetes. I say all of this, explaining my wrist dislocations, exactly how the pain feels and where the pain is. Later, I will print a picture of an outlined body and I will colour in all the places which are plagued by pain.

As I write, I think back to the torment of my last PIP assessment and my resolve to get this done, and get it done right, strengthens. And with that, I become devious and petty.

Oh, I will make my PIP assessor suffer just as much as I did.

In early 2017, when flowers started to bloom and baby rabbits began to emerge from their burrows, I put in a claim for a change of circumstances with my disability. It was true, my circumstances had changed. I was struggling more and more with cooking. I took a ridiculous number of medications and all of them together were, and still are, very hard to organise and manage. I currently take fifteen different medications, but back in 2017 I took six medications and was already struggling to manage. Some

---

9 All dialogue is from memory and, as such, is not repeated word for word as it was said.

had to be cut in half, which I found impossible to do with my numb fingertips and frustratingly small tablets. Looking after myself was becoming increasingly difficult and I found it upsetting to see the decline in my ability.

And so, I applied for a change of circumstances, hoping to get the enhanced rate of daily living. This would provide me with the money to buy more equipment which could help me with my daily living. I could, perhaps, employ someone to help me using the extra funds.

I sat in my university room and completed the form. I'd sit at my desk and cry, frustrated and upset, hating myself. Had I done something wrong to deserve this? That's what my church at home liked to suggest.

"If you prayed harder, you'd be cured." My youth leader said this to me on several occasions. It was an accusation. I wasn't faithful enough; I wasn't a good enough Christian. The guilt had been lain on me layer after layer, microaggression after microaggression.

This wasn't helped by my recent diagnosis of Type 2 Diabetes. I had been at university for a month, a fresher struggling to adapt to being a university student. I had symptoms of a urinary tract infection, something I'd had only a month previously. I put it down to the 15cm ovarian cyst which was compressing my bladder.

I booked an appointment with a nurse, pissed into a cup, and then attended my appointment. I expected antibiotics and that was all.

The nurse put the indicator stick into the cup and frowned.

"You've got glucose in your urine. Has that happened before?"

"What? No, I had a UTI last month and I didn't have glucose in my urine." My stomach churned. I knew what glucose in your urine meant. I knew it meant diabetes.[10]

---

[10] "Glucose in Urine Test: MedlinePlus Medical Test," *MedlinePlus*. U.S. National Library of Medicine, 31/07/2020, https://medlineplus.gov/lab-tests/glucose-in-urine-test/. (accessed 19/05/2021)

CANDACE PIETTE

Candace Piette was brought up in Rio de Janeiro. She joined the BBC World Service after university and did stints as the BBC's correspondent in Brazil and Argentina. She was drawn to the Amazon many times to report on illegal gold-mining and deforestation. She has also worked as the BBC's Americas desk editor.

piettecandace@gmail.com

Manaus
An essay

The captain's voice cut through the plane noise announcing in Portuguese and then English that the flight would take three hours. Brazil's dry central plateau was already giving way to the fringes of the rainforest. I felt the usual thrill that we would soon be flying over a vast ocean of green the size of western Europe. We were on course to arrive on time. The temperature at our destination, Manaus was expected to be around thirty degrees Celsius with eighty per cent humidity.

I flicked through the pages of notes in the folder on my lap. I was heading for one of the ugliest and most dilapidated towns in Brazil. I had been trying to write a book about the city for years. I wondered why I was so fascinated by it. Manaus was a concrete canker, I thought, squatting at the confluence of two major rivers, the Rio Negro and the Solimões, but somehow it seemed to be emitting a warning.

My last visit had been several years ago, to research locations and guests for a day of broadcasting on deforestation in the Amazon basin. There had been a boat trip on the Rio Negro. Manaus lying low on the horizon, high cumulous clouds rising behind it. The setting sun glancing off the port buildings in the distance as the wind whipped up, spraying my face with dark sweet river water.

The boatman cuts the speeding engine. He's seen a canoe heading towards us. I spot a boy, twelve or so, paddling with one hand and holding up a young sloth with the other, its strange cartoon face turned upwards. He drops the animal into the bottom of the canoe and rows rapidly towards the boat. Grabbing hold of the side, he picks it up by one long arm and tries to push it into my lap. I feel sudden revulsion, thinking of its fleas and ticks and its greasy fur. 'Não, não, não quero!' I shout. Thunder rumbles overhead. I fancy I can hear the bells of São Sebastião church pealing the quarter hour into the jungle. Manaus, a ludicrous cardboard cut-out on the horizon, dissolves into the darkness.

I looked down on the sunlit forest thousands of feet below out of the plane window, imagining the undulation of the land beneath the trees, their roots gripping the hills. Manaus seemed to me more of an idea than a place. I wondered if I wanted to use it as a symbol for the whole of the region's ills.

I had always been drawn to the rainforest's mystery. When I was a child at home in Rio de Janeiro, I saw television reports about a German girl, seventeen-year-old Juliane Koepcke, who was the only passenger to survive the crash of a small plane in the Peruvian jungle. After a fall of three thousand feet, she managed to free herself from the wreck of the plane seat that had protected her. Dazed and in pain, she remembered what her parents, who were scientists doing jungle field research had taught her about survival. She found a stream and followed it until she found a river. Eventually eleven days later she limped into a logging camp.

I dreamed about the story for weeks. I thought of her, I watched Juliane, stumbling through the forest alone dressed in a short cotton dress and one remaining white plastic sandal. I saw her digging the maggots from her wounds and heard her crying in the cold night rain. I imagined her hunger when the bag of boiled sweets she took from the wreckage ran out. My dreams had filled with the calls of howler monkeys and the cold fear of a jaguar emerging from the dark trees.

The air hostess was moving slowly down the aisle pushing her metal trolley before her, handing out plastic trays with sweet ham and cheese buns and coffee. Across the aisle there was chatter from a family, excited by the prospect of the visit home. The man was wearing a baseball hat and shorts in the plane's icy air conditioning and I noticed he ordered two beers for himself.

Before the trip I had trawled through stacks of notes on the nineteenth century in Manaus and the rubber boom. I was looking for a way to illustrate this key historical moment for the region, when arguably the seeds of the rainforest's destruction were sown. I had come across the story of a German photographer, George Huebner. Huebner's photographs of Manaus, published in Europe in the early nineteen-hundreds had helped attract thousands of migrants into the pristine wilderness. I glanced at a self-portrait of him, taken in 1910, showed a slight man with a neat waxed moustache wearing a white double-breasted linen suit and matching shoes. He carried a Panama hat and a black cane. George had arrived in Manaus in 1898 when the rubber boom was in full throttle and migrants were arriving by the boatload; the city had been a building site; new hotels and grand villas and municipal buildings going up everywhere. The pulse of rubber money was turning the city into "the Paris of the Tropics."

He set up a photographic studio on the grandest of Manaus's avenues, Avenida Eduardo Ribeiro, the year the city's Opera house had held its first concert. On my last visit, I had queued for an hour to get in, hoping to discover a useful location for filming. It had a magnificent stage curtain which had caught my eye. Painted in an overblown romantic style, a goddess lay attended by satyrs, bathing in the surging waters of the dark Rio Negro and the tan waters of the Solimões river join. It was Manaus herself. Tropical vegetation behind the figures formed a luxuriant green screen. The melding of white, European civilisation into the dark luxuriance of tropical forests, ripe for exploitation.

I looked around the plane. Most people were dozing or watching films. Across the aisle, three businessmen in shirts already losing their crispness guffawed at a football joke. In the seats in front, a young woman readjusted the muslin cloth draped over her nursing baby. I shivered in the icy air-conditioning and grabbed a shawl from my bag. There was a scribbled quote in the margins of my notes. It was by Werner Herzog, the German film director, from his memoir on the shooting in 1981 of his extraordinary film "Fitzcarraldo" set in the Amazon during the rubber era. He had described the Opera House as "placed in demented splendour in the middle of the rainforest by rubber millionaires at a time there was hardly a town." He had spent years shooting that film, drawn by the madness in the place. The disaster caused by the febrile lust for gold and rubber and easy riches that had brought so many people to this frontier town.

The captain's voice crackled over the intercom, announcing that soon we would be landing and that we should fasten our seatbelts.

For George Huebner, Manaus was his *El Dorado* – his golden opportunity. His studio was the first in the city and he grew prosperous photographing the rubber barons and their forest operations. One of the richest was Waldemar Scholz, a fellow German. He had been a Stuttgart provision store clerk but had made a fortune importing European goods. George would have attended his famous parties where prostitutes mostly from France or Jewish women from Eastern Europe, *'polacas'*, and *'cocotas'*, wallowed in baths of vintage champagne lapped up by excited guests.

I shivered; dark images of Manaus's greedy soul and dirty past still haunted me from the last trip. One of George Huebner's acquaintances and probably a frequent guest at Scholz's parties was the Peruvian, Julio Cesar Arana. His photograph showed a smooth face, a well-cut beard and cold arrogance. He had doubled his rubber output in three years using the labour of the Boras, the Andokes, the Ocainas, and the Huitoto people. His Peruvian Amazon Rubber Company which had been floated on the London Stock Exchange had been investigated by the British Consul in Rio de Janeiro, Roger Casement. The report he produced in 1911 contained eye-witness accounts of extreme cruelty. The terrorising of Arana's indigenous workers through starvation, drownings, hangings and the mutilation and burning alive of those who had not fulfilled their rubber harvesting quotas.

Huebner could not have avoided seeing what was going on. Perhaps he willed himself to believe that everything was correct. His photographs were a kind of green-washing, depicting rows of sad-eyed indigenous workers dressed for the camera in borrowed clean clothes.

There was another outburst of jarring laughter from the businessmen across the aisle. Europeans in Latin America have blinded themselves to horror for centuries. I thought of my own family's involvement, I realised I had never asked my father before he died if working for a British company selling power station equipment to Latin American governments in the sixties and seventies, he had had to turn a blind eye to the actions of the region's military rulers.

I was struggling with the idea that I would have to rein in my romantic clichéd notions of the place if I was to tackle Manaus's complex heritage. Like so many journalists, it had been enough to dine out for years at London parties on exotic tales of the city. I remember describing buying bowls of *tacaca*, in Manaus under the rosewood trees at a street stall in the main square in front of the Opera house. The soup was an indigenous recipe containing *mandioc*; tapioca gum, dried shrimps, small yellow peppers and *jambu* – a green vegetable that leaves a strange numbing sensation in the mouth. It had felt wild and strange and I had thrown most of it away.

There had been a strange, guilty pleasure in an encounter with an indigenous girl in a riverside restaurant who spoke no Portuguese. She sold me a necklace of exquisite tiny brown seeds while she played with her gurgling baby. I had told my friends the technicoloured version of her story and left out the deep poverty of her family on the outskirts of Manaus.

I was still smarting from a phone call I had made before the flight. I had rung Marcia Wayna Kambeba for a local perspective on what had happened in the past. A poet, writer and member of the Tikuna people, she was born in the upper reaches of the Solimões River and had studied at a university in Manaus. On a bad line to her home in a small Amazonian town, she had rejected my overture telling me bluntly she was tired of western guilt trips. 'You have a fairy-tale view of indigenous people. We are no longer 'pobres coitados' (poor things). We understand the world and are no longer victims. We fight for our rights and our territories and to not be seen from a colonial perspective.'

We were landing now. In Waldemar Scholz's garden, last time, I watched the black vultures, the *Urubus*, exquisitely soaring in the thermals above me. A strong breeze played through the giant fig tree. I imagined a whiff of Parisian cologne, a glimpse of jewels sparkling on low necklines. I half-heard a quartet, on the afternoon breeze. A servant seemed to appear at my elbow with a flute of chilled champagne but evaporated as I turn away.

Roger Casement's report atomised the dreams of Manaus's founding fathers of creating a beacon of European civilization in the wilderness. But it left little trace. After the rubber boom ended, armies of desperate poor and calculating rich streamed from the city's gates, virtually unabated, to continue their devastation of the forests and their harassment of indigenous people.

The birds above me had spiralled into the blue air. I sensed the rustle of silks and taffetas in the Amazonian evening air. I half-glimpsed the powerful men with their wives and mistresses wandering into the grand house, oblivious to the sound of weeping, floating on the air like seeds from the forest.

DAFYDD POWELL HALLS

Dafydd Powell Halls is from Abergavenny, South Wales. He is an anthropology graduate from Brunel University and works as an English as a Foreign Language teacher. He writes about the world around him.

dafphalls@hotmail.com

Clippings

Yusuf holds my hair tight between his middle and forefinger. His scissors stop, and I look up at him in the mirror. The skin is darker under his eyes, which makes him look like he's just been smoking or crying. The presence of the mirror means his intention is directed towards it rather than me and I nod in acknowledgement to his words, away from him.

I don't like football, mate. I like money. I like life. I enjoy life. I've lived in Cardiff, Liverpool, Gloucester, and Norwich. I've been to many places. I speak many languages. I speak Turkish, Russian, Macedonian – some Bulgarian too. Norwich, it's nice, but it's expensive. You know how much I pay for two bed, kitchen, bathroom, shower? It's ok though. I like work, I do this every day. I have to.

On the countertops by the mirror are tubs and bottles of soft gels and gloopy surfaces. They are all different shapes and sizes, appearing as they would in a cartoon laboratory. Behind me, I can see the worn crimson sofa, usually occupied with waiting customers, and more mirrors, reflecting the barber chairs which are like *Crème Life* boiled sweets, strawberry red and white.

Look down please.

He holds my hair as he speaks, before continuing with the layering scissors. He is talking about a tiny deer he saw in the graveyard across the road that was running over the tombstones and eating cut flowers. He hadn't been so chatty when I arrived. He had walked listlessly onto the barbershop floor led by his phone, watching someone, talking through his headphones. He said goodbye in his language, kissed his fingers, gestured them to the phone and paused for a moment as the screen went black. He'd been out the back for some time too which was strange as I know that Adem who takes the chair at the front usually calls out if there's anyone free. Yusuf had finally invited me to sit with an outstretched arm and wrapped a barber collar around my neck without a word. He checked his phone again and I waited for his attention while observing the collar which appeared to have split my body, reminding me of a whiplash patient – before the swoop of the barber cloak, and a lovely waft of air.

Adem's is the name of my barbers. I had met Adem sometime before Yusuf, when I had first moved to Norwich on my tour around the shops. It was a cold evening – the stillness outside disturbed only by the hypnotic spiral of the barber pole. I had paused to look at the price list in the window, which was cheap with the student discount. Adem opened the door for me, leaving his customer stranded with his side trim half finished. Hello mate, come on in, take a seat, we'll be right with you.

The barbershop is in a row of businesses which skirt around a carpark, built for the supermarket which dominates the skyline in front of them. The location reminds me of American strip mall, where the greatest amount of space is reserved for parking, but where the contrast of dead tarmac, the precedence given to vehicles, sharpens the life found over the thresholds that back onto them.

Adem's is between a furniture shop which gives away square pieces of carpet for free, and an Iranian man's shop selling pulses, honey, and incense but which is labelled with a faded "Ice Cream" sign of the previous occupants. There is a pleasing frame cast around the front of Adem's in the day: shelves of pansies, succulents, and a box of fennel are on one side, and rolled-up carpets, usually propped against a drainpipe on the other. Across the top, is a sheet-plastic roof with mouldy guttering for the flats above, and below are pictures of good-looking men with fresh haircuts taken from Google images. The images I know, because I've searched "short on sides long on top haircut" before and found the same ones.

I'd described that type of haircut to Yusuf when he asked me what I wanted: short on the side and with scissors on the top. We then talk, as you must, about work, home, and money. The conversation is pleasant and formal, but he appears preoccupied, the focus of his eyes shifting from cool detachment to strained and vacant. We lie about how we were doing then, which is how it works. And we're good. Always good, brother.

Each snip of the scissors complements the retelling of his stories. Falling and looking messy with flecks of dandruff accompanying them, sprinkling the creases of my gown, and resting dormant on my knees and the floor. Does he notice the snow, the hair I had neglected to wash. He talks about his girlfriend. How frustrating it is being long distance, but how different it will be once they are married. It will happen soon, he tells me. No, I was not married. He seems surprised.

He is always talking to his girlfriend, say two of the other barbers, teasing him further in another language, waving a pair of scissors and a straight razor. Yusuf is around my age, as they all could be, not so far past twenty-five. Crissh, crissh, he talks about his family. They live in Turkey. He comes from a long line of barbers: his father, his grandfather, prices at around one pound over there mate, really. There is a framed photo in front of his chair, next to the sink. It's sepia coloured of a grinning boy, next to a barber chair, outside, beneath a maple tree on the streets of Ankara. That's me man, yes, working there since I was a thirteen, that's my family's chair.

My experiences of barbershop's have been both good and bad. Recollections that return as I enter them, fusing with the same conversations and smells of hair gel. In Spain, I laughed when I came out with a quiff that kept on going: a golden statue on top of my forehead, an iced gem. I cried when, as a young boy in Cumbria, my hairdresser (misunderstanding my mother's instructions) started shaving the top of my head, exposing my white scalp – until then unseen to me – to natural light. The guilty hairdresser, the clippers thick with long strands of a 7-year-old's ginger hair looked at my mother, who in the mirror, sat with her hand over her mouth. Tears were rolling down my cheeks as the hairdresser continued shaving – the vertical lights on the wall glowing like crystal stilts, framing my mother just over my shoulder. I wore my jumper on my head for the whole next day at school, my chin hard against the desk, keeping as low as I could and the washed stiff cotton, the chewed-at-the-wrists sleeves wrapped against the short spikes, covering them. I remember my classmates asking to see what I was hiding underneath. I had attributed so much to the length of the strands on my head, and that stark baldness I knew I could never show other children.

It is strange how dull my hair looks on the floor compared with how it feels attached to my body. Once separated, it dies, transforms, and is swept off into the dark corners of the barbershop floor.

Adem's has many stories swept away. On a late Friday, with hair left too long, Adem's window was like a white flare in the gloaming. The glass was all steamed up and a pool of light stretched into the pavement. As I entered, five barbers at five chairs looked up and nodded. The long sofa was full. Men and boys, dads and sons, builders and others who weren't as easy to distinguish. Boys who seemed like they'd had haircuts already, back again, waiting on their phones. Some slumped back against the chair, staring out into the room, into the mirrors, where we all saw each other. Steam billowed out of a small machine positioned next to the barber's chair – it was softening the facial hairs of a man, sat reclined, eyes closed, with a spider's web tattooed on the top of his head. Hot towels warmed his neck and hands as the barber gently scraped the outline of his beard.

An old woman entered, just as I found a space on the sofa: white hair, white skin in a pink jumper and blue jeans. Ay, how you been, said Adem. I'm well, well as can be. Look at the state of this place. I can see you've been busy. She took a broom and swept the hairs and tissues scattered across the floor. She swept a few tissues of blood dropped by the barber who was dabbing a customer's chin. You going to sing us a song today, asked a man with scissors, and she turned to him with a grin. With the broom handle she posed like Freddy Mercury and began a mumbled croon. She moved her shoulders, slowly. A father next to me started smiling – some of the boys looking startled, others didn't pay attention. She sang for a few seconds, then lowered her broom and continued sweeping.

She turned to me, leaning over, like she was sharing a secret. I got a new jumper today, from the charity shop, price tag was still on it, how do you think it looks? I feel marvellous in it. I haven't bought new clothes in years. I smiled in response, giving a nod of appreciation to the inner world, however brief, she'd given me. She returned to the room. Right lads, that's me done for the day. You'll have to empty this bin, it's full, I can only take it so far. Have a good night, see you. See you my dear. And it was back to the mirrors.

Yusuf stops his cutting again. The pause allows me to raise my eyes to him. I got to make enough money, you know. I have to pay dowry, £15,000, brother, in gold. I thought that dowries worked differently, but you don't question these things. I just hope there's no more lockdowns, I need the shop open, a whole year of doing nothing. I've got to work. I think of the weight of gold: each lock of hair, thousands, tens of thousands, cut, slicked, brushed, blown and swept out and away.

He presents a mirror behind me, and I see the back of my head, revealing my neck with the acne scars and off coloured spots. Darker purples against a red neck, shaven closely to the skin. I don't like seeing it. That's great, I say, thank you. I do think the haircut looks good, better, though I can never decide if I should keep my hair short or long. I get my coat and fumble in my pockets for change, the warm back pocket, twenty pounds, and it's twelve but I say give me five back because of the dowry. Thank you, mate. I step out into the cool evening. I am suddenly aware of my ears, and the touches of wind on the skin beneath them.

JUDY REITH

Judy Reith is a writer and life coach specialising in family relationships, ageing and widowhood. She is writing a memoir about her parents' turbulent marriage, a novel about widows chasing a silver fox, and a confessional piece to her late husband about the last four days of his life.

judy@act3life.com

Gone

In November 2021, Adrian, my husband of 32 years died of cancer. This is my first attempt to turn that hideous time into a legacy that encompasses my truth of losing him, which only my diary knew about at the time. I found it impossible to know where to start, or how to write it, so eventually I decided to just stop fretting, and write, and see what came out. This is an extract from the last 4 days of his life.

One morning last October, I took you a cup of tea in bed. Not my bed by then. I hadn't slept beside you since 12th Night when we took down the Christmas tree. As I tip-toed in, I said good morning in my sing-song voice, my heart quickening at what I might find today.

'Hello darling,' you croaked as I left your tea on the bedside table, the one that used to be mine, but now you need the nearest route to the en-suite for the multiple overnight interruptions that come with your disease.

'Beautiful day,' I said, easing open the putty striped curtains and stepping aside so you could see the long view across dozens of back gardens. Breakfast sunshine beamed from the cloudless sky over the trees, hedges and lawns showing off their autumnal feast of yellows, russets and fading greens. I sat at the foot of our bed and studied your face, almost as familiar to me as my own. You were propped up on four pillows, one the shape of a boomerang and I made a mental note it needed a clean pillowcase. You blinked, the sunlight catching the green in your hazel eyes. Your salt and pepper clammy hair in shards on your forehead with cheeks blotched pink from your unruly internal thermostat. Beside you was the old red washing up bowl that had shared the bed with you for a week, left within reach, along with a tired out towel we'd had since the girls were small.

'How was the night?' I asked, eyebrows up, a nod to the empty bowl.

'Not bad. Couple of trips to the loo.'

I reached across and stroked your veiny hand. Your skin felt warm, flaky, in need of hand cream. There was enough hand cream in the house to moisturise all the hands in Cambridge. Since January, we had been deluged with love gifts sent from friends and family, wanting to help, but unable to visit. We had to keep you Covid safe as your immune system was shot from chemotherapy. It was as if the house was wrapped in P.P.E. with the volume of masks, hand washing, and lateral flow testing that went on. Every time the doorbell rang Ted barked and circled the rug chasing his tail, making us all jump. The postman and I are on first name terms because of all the chocolates, doughnuts, fruit, books, magazines, paintings, poems, even a foot spa that joined the piles of hand cream. When a box of frozen herrings arrived from Holland, I was reminded of that line in John Betjeman's Christmas poem, 'hideous tie so kindly meant'. They made you gag.

Flowers became a dilemma. Fresh, bright, scented riots of colour delivered in boxes with typed messages, 'Thinking of you' being the number one greeting while 'Holding you in the light' was the favoured one from our church going friends. We were stumped by 'All my love, Jane xxx'. Which Jane? We know four. Vases and jugs of blooms filled the house, as they did when our babies were born. When I remembered, I left a posy in a bud vase beside the bathroom basin. You said you loved to see it there, a flash of beauty amongst the cardboard packs of medications to get your bowels working, or not.

'More bloody flowers,' I muttered one morning bringing in yet another delivery. You looked up at me, frowning, and said it was very kind of people to think of us. I didn't reply. On days when my caring batteries are flat, I can't see the kindness. I swear at the orange pollen stain on my cream T Shirt. I scowl at the flower water morphing into a mucus slime that smells sour and rotten. I see vases of wilting blooms dying in front of me. On brighter days, I whip round snipping stems, refreshing the water and sprinkling in that white powdery flower food. I double check the vase you gaze at from your kitchen armchair will be a source of joy.

There was something about you that morning that was hard to define. You seemed a little more like your old self, as if you had had a kind of energy reboot overnight. I witnessed an uplift in your strength as you shifted and heaved your upper body before softening your back into the pillow nest. You caught my eye as you reached over for your mug of tea.

'It's lovely to see you.' I heard myself say.

'It's always lovely to see you,' you replied, a smile playing on your thinning lips. I locked those words in my memory, with the image of you sitting up in bed, in your Marks and Spencer navy polka dot pyjamas, downsized to medium, sipping tea. It was a memory that soothed and sustained me in what turned out to be your last month. It was as if I could believe the philosopher Blaise Pascal's words *'In difficult times, always keep something beautiful in your mind,'* when hope had long gone. Alone now, the memory recurs as a daydream, or haunts me in the darkest hours as I wait for daybreak.

NOVEMBER 26TH

Supper time. I arrive with our daughter Tilly, Ted and a chiller bag of your favourite cheese, Baron Bigod, just as delicious as Brie, but made in Suffolk. There is a bottle of Mucho Mas, a Spanish red that you discovered last winter over a beef stew with friends, and promptly bought a case. We will eat this picnic off our laps in the recliner chairs that circle your bed as if we were in an old people's home. Except this is the Arthur Rank Hospice, a place for those whose days are numbered, usually in single digits. We were told this morning by the duty doctor, a pin thin woman who spoke in slow whispers that you have too many complications now to take you home. For you, this was a final unwanted bulletin in ten months of bad news about Boris. That's what you named your tumour as you said you hadn't voted it in, and you were doing everything possible to vote it out. I watched your face slump with disappointment, but I could feel my relief, like air escaping from a tyre, that the skilled hands of the hospice would hold us all until your last breath. There would be no delivery of a hospital bed, or bags of medicines and feeding paraphernalia taking over our sitting room. I was fearful of your last days at home with the girls and I keeping watch like floundering Florence Nightingales, while we tried to stop Ted barking. Although gut punched with guilt, I was quietly convinced that home needed to remain a place of respite from the hospice for us, where we returned to be energised by a hot shower, nourished by a meal without you watching us eat, or just some mindless scrolling through WhatsApp. I was prepared to bring you home if the doctor had allowed it, but her decision was mercifully clear. Bring home here, she said.

So we did. We stuffed the car with your favourite armchair, two standard lamps, a reading light, the obligatory flowers, the dog, and a framed photo of all of us taken in the garden after a sunny lunch in lockdown. Having arranged these tokens of home amongst the standard issue hospice room bed and recliner chairs, the nurses oohed and ahhhed at our efforts. You nodded your approval at this aesthetic upgrade. In all the places we have lived, making a practical and welcoming home environment has always been important to both of us. But your critic's eyes and ears never stopped noticing where we placed furniture, or hung the art, or brightened gloomy corners with cosy lamps. Whatever was played from our expensive sound system caused you to comment, or tweak the levels, or simply switch it off. I loved this creative gift of yours, but not at the expense of the inhabitants, especially visitors. In the infancy of our marriage, we had invited friends round to supper. You were upstairs when they arrived, so I showed them into the kitchen and poured the drinks as small talk drifted between us. When you appeared, you took no notice of our guests and instead announced that the lighting was all wrong and you then proceeded to dart about you then proceeded to dart about switching on and off various lamps and overhead lights. We have argued about lighting versus greeting guests ever since. But tonight, we ease you into your armchair and wiggle your feet into your slippers. You smile at us sitting in the warm light of lamps from home.

Tilly pulls out the picnic items one by one with a flourish, like rabbits out of a magician's hat. She makes up small plates of cheese, oatcakes, grapes and chutney. You haven't eaten anything that could be called a meal for weeks. On some days, you attempt a spoonful or two of yoghurt, a few sips of tea. Yesterday afternoon you sat up in bed licking a yellow ice lolly like a child. They continue to feed you overnight with the liquid food supplement that pumps straight into your lower intestine. It's like the consistency of thick cream, a dhal coloured odourless gloop that has kept you alive since surgery took out your oesophagus in July. There was a smattering of days when you could manage toddler sized meals, mushed into soft lumps but that's a distant memory now. I stare at my plate so thoughtfully arranged by Tilly as she passes me a china mug of wine. I'm unsure if we should be eating such a selection of goodies in front of you. But I am reminded how you have said repeatedly, all year, when swallowing and eating became so difficult for you, that we should carry on as normal. You said you didn't want Boris to spoil our enjoyment of food and drink.

   Tilly sat down and began to spread oozing cheese on an oatcake.
   'Don't I get a plate?' you said.
   'Of course, Dad,' she replied, jumping up.' Fancy some wine too?'
   'Why not?' you said. I can't be sure, but I think you looked at me and winked.

You managed a few mouthfuls of what turned out to be your last supper. We spent the next hour selecting songs off Spotify you wanted played at your funeral. During Talking Heads "Take Me To The River" we cranked up the volume and sang along like a pub crowd, recreating a family habit formed over years of long car journeys and kitchen discos. Just as well the very old lady in the room next door was unconscious. You reclined in your chair, Ted at your feet, and taking part *almost* as if there was nothing wrong. We teetered on the edge of just another rowdy family Friday night, warmed by food and drink and messing around with songs on the laptop. I don't know how we did it. I suspect the Mucho Mas had a part to play.

TINA ROCCHIO

Tina Marisa Rocchio grew up in Vermont but has spent her adult life in Italy. Her writing explores family ties and intergenerational trauma with humor and poignancy. Fascinated by place, identity and belonging, Tina's profound understanding of Italian culture comes across in her observations of Italians and their daily life.

tmrocchio@gmail.com

Prolonging Loss

There is such a thing as anticipatory grief. It holds you in its grip for as long as the terminal disease lasts. Dementia grief waxes and wanes as your daily life moves forward, worsening as the symptoms do, as you mourn your loved one bit by bit. You are captive in no man's land. You're grief-stricken but also caring, sometimes hoping, other times denying. Throes of love and passion, of belly-aching laughter with friends come less frequently. You harden. You wonder if the clouds will ever part. You wonder if this pre-grief is worse than grief itself. The natural cycle of loss is more linear; as painful as it is, there is loss, there is grief, there is moving past grief. In prolonged, anticipatory grief the sadness lingers. Sometimes for years, decades even. It brings families together; it tears families apart. There are infinite ways to tell this tale; this is but one.

THE OTHER GUY

Following his diagnosis in 2011, my father had several good years. He was able to drive and function, masking his lapses with humor and deflection. He exercised daily, ate walnuts, seeds, turmeric, and other said-to-be-brainy foods. He played word games and challenged everyone at his post-retirement job in the Dartmouth gym to the daily scramble.

During this phase, notes spelled out phonetically and cards ill-aligned in Solitaire struck like a gut punch. If we bumped into someone Dad knew whom he had trouble placing, he'd point to me and smile, "There's something going on with me. Talk to her, she's terrific. Tell him, honey." And I would. Pats on the back and conversations would ensue and be forgotten before we got to the car.

Food and football became unimportant for the ultimate home chef and legendary coach that was my dad. His appetite never waned but his Stanley Tucci-like zest for flavors and memories tied to homecooked Italian food dissipated like salt on an Amalfi lemon.

The last football game we saw together was on a freezing October afternoon six years ago. Dartmouth was playing Harvard at home. My brother, a former football player, kept trying to engage Dad in the game. Instead, Dad was happily fixated on the visiting team's band in the stands with their cymbals and trumpeters. "Look at them! Aren't they terrific?" While I enjoyed laughing with Dad each time a drummer drummed, my brother was crushed; their football connection was no longer.

The filters began to fall away. Thoughts he never would have vocalized surfaced and poured out of his unfettered mind as we drove down to my sister's; things he used to deem too heavy for me to hold are now lodged in my brain. When it's not emotionally devastating, it's fascinating to see thoughts unravel like endless spools of thread, not only open but vulnerable to the interpretation of the listener; it's like a decade-long game of Telephone. Ever the philosopher, as language falls away, profundity remains. In a video I made in 2019, the man whose license plate always asked "WHY" mused, "Who wins? Who needs? Who has to? Make sure the whole world is together."

Over the years Dad has progressively slipped away into his mind, a baffling web of firing synapses that alternately entertain, confuse, and throw us into despair. As he sinks deeper, his dashing blue eyes reveal another self: "the Other Guy," I call him. We love the Other Guy and posit that our father would, too. He's as happy as he is unaware.

In the summer of 2021, I arrived at his home in Vermont after nearly two years of forced separation due to the pandemic. Like many, I had been Corona-catapulted into joblessness. Alone in my loft in Rome with no balconies to sing from, I took pride in my 7000 steps per day (that's 62 steps from the door to the furthest window roughly 112 times). I amassed fantastic playlists; created a Virtual Decameron[1] on Facebook; sorted through old letters. I cooked and cleaned. I followed the government's daily press conferences and published a series of articles on the situation in my corner of Italy for my hometown newspaper. I did yoga and meditation online. I resisted bingeing on series and snacks. It would only be upon exiting this heightened state of emergency that I would begin to feel the traumatic effects of lockdown. For the first time in my life, I was packed and ready to go several days before our flight back to the US.

When I walked into my dad's dining room, I hugged his wife, taking care not to crush her slight frame. We'd seen each other only on FaceTime

---

[1] www.facebook.com/groups/239164223779075 The VirtualDecameron was based on Boccaccio's 14th Century collection of short stories. Our group of 125 members submitted art and stories, songs, and memories around a daily theme.

during the pandemic. Distance and isolation had taken their toll. Dad hardly looked up from his drawing.

For several years now he has drawn colorful patterns with Sharpies in such repetitive linear strokes that he has a permanent open sore on the side of his right pinky, his blood sometimes fusing with the colors on the paper. The beguiling color combinations and shapes have replaced the poetry and prose that once flowed so easily. In a way these thousands of drawings comprise the Great American Novel my dad composed in his mind over a lifetime but was too inhibited to write. Inhibitions banished, the Other Guy takes immense pride in his art.

When he finishes, he looks up at us. My daughter is with me. He holds up his drawing and asks, "you like that? Isn't it terrific?" before taking another blank page and starting all over again. He is unfazed by our presence, just as he was unfazed by our long absence.

I'm reminded of the one time I let more than a year go by without returning home. At the time, he took me aside and said, "don't ever let that much time go by again." That was my father. The Other Guy doesn't know his daughter is in the room. The filial concept eludes him now, the only relation he recognizes is his wife (whom he calls Mommy), and that between himself and his mother and father whom he is utterly convinced await him.

Later that same afternoon, he'll grab my hand and look me in the eye, "You'll take me home, right? You know they're waiting for me." Then he'll look suspiciously at the others in the room and whisper behind his hand, so they won't see, "Let's go!" Throughout the summer, this pattern repeats itself, often several times an hour. Sometimes pleading, sometimes agitated, occasionally aggressive.

When it gets really bad, when not even the newest, brightest Sharpies are able to "redirect him," I put him in the car telling him I'll take him home. I wind up and down the dirt roads with him next to me. As he looks around, he speaks to me in fuller sentences than usual, raising my hopes with a clarifying, "The thing is…" But then, sadly, the thing escapes us both. He mimics my opening of the window by doing the same on his side. "Hey, look at that! You put that there, so I put mine there, too," he exclaims victoriously. By "that" he means air and by "there" he means the space where the window used to be.

Bored with windows, he discovers a pristine paper towel, folded several times over, in his pocket. He takes it out, unfolds it and shows it to me. "Isn't it terrific? I keep it right here. I have others, too." He fastidiously folds it back up and puts it back in his pocket. The fixation with paper towels started several years ago. Once, when I took him for hot cocoa at a local country store, he had to use the restroom. Back then he could go in on his own as long as someone stood outside the door. When he was done washing his hands, he opened the door and excitedly whispered to me, "hey, come take a look at what I found!" There on its own holder was a new roll of paper towels. "Isn't that terrific? You want one? Take one. They won't mind."

As I drive, the man who has replaced my dad reaches for my hand and takes it in his own. He kisses the back of my hand, my wrist, my forearm, turning my hand over again and again between both of his. I am reluctant to take it back but more reluctant to drive off the mountain, so I place it back on the steering wheel. He's happy. He has no idea who I am, but he knows I am important to him. When we've driven a 45-minute loop of backroads, I signal to turn. "Where are we going now?" he asks. "Home," I say. "You wanted me to take you home. Here we are."

"Oh, goody. Thank you, thank you."

OUR FATHER

Our father believes that literature is the ultimate mirror to the human condition, "and what are we, after all, if not conditioned humans?"

Our father quotes Shakespeare, William Faulkner, and Yogi Berra in equal measure. Through him, all those in his orbit learned to laugh and see each other as "just players on a stage."

He's a first-generation degree seeker, a second generation Italian-American, a War Veteran and a maverick from a family of builders who got his Master's in English Literature on the GI Bill.

He exalts intellect and the imagination, warns of the evils of ego, and extols the virtues of forgiveness, empathy, peaceful cohabitation.

Our father is always working on his unfinished manuscript. He jots down poems on cocktail napkins and could fill a book of original aphorisms.

He promises always to spend more time, try harder, be more connected, more present.

He procrastinates. Profusely.

He's quick-witted and irreverent. To our "Oh my God!" he responds, "yes, my child?" To "Oh God, Dad," he replies, "that's redundant."

His laughter and joke-telling enliven the room. At every family event, his table is inevitably *the* table.

AWAY AGAIN

I walk around the little hamlet of Ringland where I'm living - just east of Norwich in the County of Norfolk, England - decluttering my mind so the ideas jockeying for a position on the page arrange themselves in an orderly line. The ruralness of it reminds me of childhood in Vermont; even after so many years of living in Rome, retreat to silence and the dark of night comes naturally to me. My dad's procrastination coupled with some deep-rooted questions of self-esteem mean that he will never be widely read. This year spent writing in the company of other writers is an attempt to reverse that pattern. I carry him with me on all my walks, my exploratory drives, as I cook, when I cheat at Solitaire. He is ever-present during this remarkable year, a gift from the uncertainty brought on by the pandemic. It's as if we're writing together.

Just recently, my family reached another phase, one of the last phases to this prolonged grief. My father was placed in a special 'memory care' unit of a nursing home. He is safe and his needs tended to while his wife and caregiver gradually remembers how to eat, drink and sleep again. He stands less tall. His range of movement is challenged, and he's a bit groggier. But his twinkle and charm remain. The day after taking him in, my older sister wrote: "Yesterday went a bit better than expected. One of the nurses told him he was handsome, and he responded, 'Tell me more.'"

EZRA JOHN WOODGER

Ezra Woodger is a UK-based writer whose interests include identity, performance, and masculinity. As one of the winners of JKP's Writing Prize, he is featured in the anthology work *Transitions: Our Stories of Being Trans*, and his debut book – *To be a Trans Man: Our Stories of Transition, Acceptance, and Joy* – is scheduled for release 21st October 2022.

@theezrajohn
ezrawoodger@gmail.com

INT. LIFE – DAY

INT. BEDROOM – DAY

A young man sits up in bed, sunlight streaming through the gaps in the curtains. He fumbles for his glasses, slides them over his nose. EZRA (white male, 20s) runs a hand through his hair, which is sticking up at all angles. He has the stubble of someone who hasn't bothered to shave for several days, but is otherwise reasonably handsome. Eyebrows from his father, cheekbones from mum.

His room is tidy enough for such a small space. A desk, chest of drawers, all the same shade of flat-pack white. There are books stacked on every surface, and the glass of water beside the bed has the soft, stagnant layer of filmy dust that settles overnight regardless of how clean a room may be. He reaches for it, groaning, and takes a gulp.

                EZRA
Ugh.

He reaches down under the desk to a small shelf and pulls out a box of pills. He pops one out of the film and swallows it with a mouthful of old water.

                EZRA
              (frowning)
Wait, what?

Apologies. EZRA reaches down under the desk to a small shelf and pulls out a box of pills. He pops one out of the foil, snaps it in half, and swallows it with another mouthful of old water. He places the remaining half carefully back into the packet.

> EZRA
> Right. Yeah.

He gets to his feet and makes the bed before studying himself in the mirror. He pulls the baggy pyjama shirt over his head to reveal a thin torso, with a pair of light pink scars running across his pectorals. He traces them lightly, a flicker of emotion crossing his face. Is it joy? Or something more complex?

> EZRA
> ...It's joy.

We cannot be sure.

INT. NURSERY - DAY

A small nursery is held in a room on the side of a local church in Buckhurst Hill, a town on the outskirts of London.

> EZRA
> Zone 5, it still counts.

A group of small children are playing dress-up. One LITTLE GIRL is pulling on an explosion of white tulle and sequins. A YOUNG EZRA is clutching her chubby hand in his own. A tiny VICAR, ordained a few minutes before with a whirl of a purple polyester cloak, stands tall and serious.

                    VICAR
          Do you take this woman to be
          your lawfully wedded wife?

The playhouse is silent, rapt.

                    YOUNG EZRA
          I do.

                    VICAR
          And do you take this man to be
          your lawfully wedded husband?

                    LITTLE GIRL
          I do.

The pair kiss, or do something that seems the
closest approximation to what small children think
a kiss is. They press their sticky lips together
before dissolving into giggles. They all tumble from
the playhouse and onto the carpet.

A parent appears, looming. DAD (white male, 30s)
towers over the group, dark eyes growing darker and
more terrifying as he pushes past the nursery staff
to where the children play.

                    DAD
              (shouting)
          What do you think you're doing?

                    YOUNG EZRA
          I- I don't-

                    DAD
          Where's your dress?

                    YOUNG EZRA
                      (tearfully)
                    I don't like dresses.

                    DAD
                    I don't care.

EZRA pushes past into the scene, rather rudely.

                    EZRA
                    What do you mean, 'rudely'? It
                    didn't happen like this at all.

Maybe it did, maybe it didn't.

                    EZRA
                      (gesturing to younger self)
                    Quite clearly it didn't, I'm
                    right there.

Can't you just let me tell a story?

                    EZRA
                    It's my story! I'm telling you,
                    it didn't happen like this
                    at all. If we're telling my
                    story, you have to show us what
                    actually happened.

Oh, you think so? Fine.

INT. LIVING ROOM- NIGHT

A large living room with a wood burning fireplace and French doors which look out onto a garden backing onto fields. The sun has long since gone down, and the room is dark. TEEN EZRA sits alone on one sofa, MUM (white woman, 40s) and DAD sit together on the other.

> MUM
> We've just had a call from the school.

Once again, EZRA makes an unexpected, intrusive entrance.

> EZRA
> Oh, no. No, fuck this, actually.

Excuse me?

> EZRA
> What are we doing here?

EZRA was looking for something that actually happened. So we find ourselves in a small village on the outskirts of Stowmarket, Suffolk. The room is dark-

> EZRA
> (interrupting)
> No. This isn't the part worth showing.

It's the part everyone wants to see, though.

> EZRA
> I don't want to see it. He doesn't want to see it.

He points at TEEN EZRA, small and pale, with thumbs sticking out the holes cut in his school jumper.

INT. LIFE- DAY - 81

              EZRA
          Ezra stands in front of his
          younger parents, almost
          defensively.

What are you doing?

              EZRA
          (pushes them out of frame
          and folds his arms)
          I don't understand why you want
          us to see them like this. It's
          been years, why bring it up
          again?

            STAGE DIRECTIONS
          Because that's what people want
          to see.

Why? Why can't we see something different?

            STAGE DIRECTIONS
          Then what would make you
          interesting?

EZRA's younger family awkwardly exit the scene.

            STAGE DIRECTIONS
          It isn't my fault that's how it
          works.

It shouldn't be.

            STAGE DIRECTIONS
          Then why do you still think
          about it?

You mean the real stuff.

>   STAGE DIRECTIONS
>   (sheepishly)
>   Yes. Well, we can all get
>   carried away.

When we started this, it was going to be a narrative people could understand. I don't remember seeing trans people just waking up, going about their day in whatever body they had.

>   STAGE DIRECTIONS
>   That's why I tried to make it
>   sadder-

With the full dose of meds, yes, I noticed. Look, I know the questions everyone asks when you tell them. It would be a lot cleaner if I could say exactly when I knew, exactly if my parents accepted me. But, instead, it's been a very long time, and I'm an adult now. I'm an adult who makes choices. My parents were adults who made choices. And now we're making choices, both separately and together.

EXT. UNIVERSITY OF SOUTHAMPTON CAMPUS- DAY

The outside of Glen Eyre Halls are green, almost brilliantly so on the summer day. There are young adults with their parents chatting to Open Day tour guides, asking questions and receiving polite, if rather imprecise, answers. The buildings curve to match the soft incline of the grassy hills, as though the architects thought sharp edges may scare away potential intake.

YA EZRA stands looking vaguely lost, wearing a loose fitting t-shirt and a jacket covered in patches and pins. DAD is here, alongside a boyfriend who will last approximately 4 days into fresher's week.

DAD notices someone wearing a staff uniform and approaches. YA EZRA and his boyfriend jog to catch up.

> DAD
> Excuse me. I was wondering
> if you could help. My son is
> interested in attending-

YA EZRA stops paying attention to the conversation. He's grinning too much. The term will never get old, no matter how many times he hears it.

The truth, it seems, or the attempt to capture the vague approximation of it, requires a degree of selfishness. When honesty becomes a performance, it ceases to be. It would, of course, be rather cinematic to explore the inner workings of a suicidal teenager, because everything inside a suicidal teenager is cinematic. We become life-or-death, swooning, fainting melodrama. I could pick out the interesting parts and make me sound miserable.

EXT. QUIET STREET- DAY

TEEN EZRA and his friend, DANIEL (white male, 18, hair thinning prematurely) sit on a low wall together. TEEN EZRA rolls a cigarette and licks it closed, fingers still unpractised and clumsy. DANIEL shields his eyes from the sun and kicks a pebble with the toe of his smart black shoes.

> TEEN EZRA
> I'm going to kill myself when
> I'm 28.

DANIEL blinks. A beat.

> DANIEL
> What?

> TEEN EZRA
> (shrugging)
> Yeah. I'll kill myself before I
> get ugly.

> DANIEL
> But that means you're basically
> already middle aged.

> TEEN EZRA
> (exhaling smoke)
> Yeah.

By those numbers, I only have a few years left. I wonder what that birthday is going to be like, watching the clock tick down to midnight. I might feel vaguely smug, I suppose. Ha, you depressed bastard. I beat you. Or maybe it'll just be a little sad. Still so young, and I thought this was all the time I was allowed? I haven't even started.

When I talk about my transition, I'm carefully carving out a chronology depending on the audience. Start with the nursery scene- as it actually happened, mind you, with parents and staff chuckling affectionately- and plot the coordinates from there. Little boy to bigger boy to fully actualised adult man. Had I only had the words, we could have seen the signs earlier. You'd be a fool not to see who I would become. Maybe that's true. But in becoming the

INT. LIFE- DAY - 85

poster boy for transgender children, I disrespect myself and my history.

INT. LIVING ROOM- DAY

(Author's note: the events depicted in this scene have been fictionalised, as the author was not present and finds it rather painful to discuss. Names and pronouns that are no longer useful have been redacted to respect the privacy of those involved).

A large living room with a wood burning fireplace and French doors which look out onto a garden backing onto fields. MUM has just got home from work and is preparing to pick up her children from school.

The landline phone rings.

          MUM
Hello?

The voice of the HEAD OF YEAR for EZRA and his brother's high school.

          HEAD OF YEAR (O.S.)
Hello, is this Mrs. Woodger?

          MUM
Speaking.

          HEAD OF YEAR (O.S.)
I wanted to have a chat with you about [REDACTED]. [REDACTED] came to see me today with some information I think you should be made aware of.

> MUM
> Is [REDACTED] alright? Safe?

> HEAD OF YEAR (O.S.)
> Yes, fine. [REDACTED] told me today that [REDACTED] wishes to use the disabled toilet, as [REDACTED] doesn't identify in a way that would fit the girl's bathroom. I said I would look into it.

Thoughts flood into MUM's head. She wasn't the first person he told. He told this stranger instead. Thoughts of betrayal. Chaz Bono. Ace fucking Ventura.

> MUM
> Thank you for letting me know. I will speak to [REDACTED] tonight.

The STAGE DIRECTIONS reappear and regard MUM for a moment.

> STAGE DIRECTIONS
> So that's what I was missing.

Yes. It's always what we were missing. It's always 'what did your parents say?' and never 'maybe your parents were put in an impossible situation when they weren't ready and neither were you'.

> STAGE DIRECTIONS
> I'm sorry.

Me too.

I wanted to give a narrative you could understand.

INT. LIFE- DAY – 87

So did you. It would be easier to put on a show
about a tortured soul trapped in the wrong body.
It would be equally as easy to take the role of
empowered transsexual wonderboy, beloved by parents
and friends alike. But it seems, in most cases,
I'm both. And neither. And memory is just a series
of bullshit excuses for how I react to things that
would, in truth, make for an awful film. None of it
makes sense, and we're lying all the time.

                STAGE DIRECTIONS
That's a terrible message to
end on.

                EZRA
   (grinning)
I know. And thank fuck for that.

ACKNOWLEDGEMENTS

This anthology contains work by the 2022 cohort of UEA's MA in Biography and Creative Non-Fiction. We are grateful to the UEA School of Literature, Drama and Creative Writing in partnership with Egg Box Publishing, without whom this anthology would not have been possible.

Many thanks to Philip Langeskov, Nathan Hamilton, and Emily Benton for your help managing and designing the anthologies, as well as your patience and willingness to answer all our inquiring emails. Thanks also to every member of the 2022 Editorial Committee, with a special shoutout to our editors – Sara Katschka, Karina Cheah, and Hannah Murgatroyd – for your time and diligence.

We would like to extend our gratitude to Andrew Kenrick and Freya Dean of Hinterland Magazine, for their generosity in contributing the foreword to our anthology.

We would also like to thank our course tutors Helen Smith, Keiron Pim, and Ian Thomson, whose insights and guidance have been invaluable in shaping our writing.

Finally, a huge thank you to our fellow students for the laughs, friendship, kindness, and workshop notes you have given us. Here's to you, to keeping in touch, and to your future writing.

UEA MA Creative Writing Anthologies: Non-Fiction

First published by Egg Box Publishing, 2022
Part of the UEA Publishing Project Ltd.

International © retained by individual authors

This book is sold subject to the condition that it shall not, by way of trade or otherwise, be lent, resold, hired out, stored in a retrieval system, or otherwise circulated without the publisher's prior consent in any form of binding or cover other than that in which it is published and without a similar condition including this condition being imposed on the subsequent purchaser.

A CIP record for this book is available from the British Library
Printed and bound in the UK by Imprint Digital

Designed by Emily Benton Book Design
emilybentonbookdesign.co.uk

Distributed by NBN International
10 Thornbury Road
Plymouth
PL6 7PP
+44 (0)1752 202 301
e.cservs@nbninternational.com

ISBN 978-1-913861-79-7